Anti-Judaism on the Way from Judaism to Christianity

Wiener Vorlesungen: Forschungen

Herausgegeben für die Kulturabteilung der Stadt Wien
von Hubert Christian Ehalt

Band 5

The differing beliefs that emerged between Christianity and Judaism, especially in the first two centuries AD, were mainly caused by the introduction of heavenly beings in the Jewish religion. This resulted in the predominance of a messiah, who will be sent by God as salvator mundi. Mainly Paul preached and practiced the conversion of pagans to Christianity, without obligating them to practice the Jewish law. In the course of time the baptized pagans represented the mainstream of Christianity which caused a conflict between them and those Jews who practiced the Jewish law but also believed in Jesus as the Messiah. The development of these tendencies is described in this book.

Peter Landesmann, born 1929 in Vienna; 1952 graduate engineer at the University of Natural Resources and Life Sciences, Vienna; 1994 PhD in Judaic Studies; 2001 Doctor of Protestant Theology; since 2006 Honorary Professor for Jewish Studies, 2007 Doctor of Catholic Theology; publication of several books and articles on Theology and related subjects.

PETER LANG

Frankfurt am Main · Berlin · Bern · Bruxelles · New York · Oxford · Wien

Peter Landesmann

Anti-Judaism on the Way from Judaism to Christianity

PETER LANG
Internationaler Verlag der Wissenschaften

Bibliographic Information published by the Deutsche Nationalbibliothek
The Deutsche Nationalbibliothek lists this publication in the Deutsche Nationalbibliografie; detailed bibliographic data is available in the internet at http://dnb.d-nb.de.

cover design:
Hubert Christian Ehalt

Translated by Wendy Jane Jones.

Printed with support
of the City of Vienna, Chief Executive Office
for European and International Affairs

ISSN 1437-9015
ISBN 978-3-631-62132-5

© Peter Lang GmbH
Internationaler Verlag der Wissenschaften
Frankfurt am Main 2012
All rights reserved.

www.peterlang.de

Wiener Vorlesungen at Vienna City Hall

Since early 1987, Wiener Vorlesungen have been inviting renowned intellectuals to present their analysis and findings on the major problems facing the world today. The presentations take place in the state rooms of Vienna City Hall. The series started with a presentation by the renowned German sociologist Professor Dr René König on the relationship between towns and universities. The analysis of this relationship and the wish to create a broad and vibrant interface between the academic public and the urban public is one of the driving forces behind the efforts of the City of Vienna to promote academic excellence, and has been put into practice with far more than 1,000 events and over 3,500 speakers who have presented their findings to an audience of more than 500,000 to date. The Wiener Vorlesungen are flanked by nine series of books. This book by Peter Landesmann is being published in the series "Wiener Vorlesungen. Research", which aims to advance and embed topics addressed by the Wiener Vorlesungen into the ongoing research discourse.

The objective of the Wiener Vorlesungen is to advance the project of enlightenment. The issue is not just knowledge as information; it is knowledge as a challenge and criticism, both of which help to further develop "education" as the individual and collective quality of knowledge and enlightenment. "Sapere aude", the peril of knowledge, as a responsible and courageous attitude and action against entrenched and ritualized conventions, is the central posit of the Wiener Vorlesungen, just as it was among the precursors of enlightenment in the 18th century. The philosophy and methodology of the project can be summarized in eight points. Enlightenment instead of obscurity, differentiation instead of simplification, analysis instead of infotainment, depth of focus instead of surface polish, empathy instead of egomania, utopia instead of continuation, contradiction instead of accommodation, challenge instead of indoctrination. The world as it stands today needs criticism and perspective in the context of this program. As the problems we are facing today in connection with the current economic and bank crises very clearly show we need to re-think business, society, politics and culture. Carrying on with our routine is no longer possible: This fact has, in recent years, become clearer than ever before.

Irrespective of the difficult political, ideological and highly complex thematic concept behind the Wiener Vorlesungen, which currently criticize the socially and economically powerful theory that the world is a corporation whose success is dictated solely by the market, the concept of the Wiener Vorlesungen is clear and simple: Renowned intellectuals put up for discussion their analyses and assessment of origins and approaches to overcome the critical problems facing the world today. Since 1987 the Wiener Vorlesungen have been drawing a rich and multi-faceted picture of the contemporary social and intellectual situation in close sequence and to an audience that is constantly growing. What makes this project so fascinating is that it manages, time and again, to attract a very large audience to presentations offering challenging insights, and that they do not only listen, but also join in the discussions. The Wiener Vorlesungen turn Vienna City Hall, which is home to local decision-making and public administration, from a center of politics and administration into a city university. The audience comes from all segments of the city's population; very many participants come from the university and college sector, of course, but what is so important about this project is that just as many Viennese come to the presentations who would otherwise not take part in academic events. They come because they identify with Vienna City Hall as the place that deals with their affairs. Their very presence strengthens the democratic character of the building.

Time and again, the series has succeeded in attracting high-level speakers such as Nobel Laureates and winners of Alternative Nobel Prizes, who have enriched science and profession with their ability to shatter clichés and to look far beyond the boundaries of their discipline. What also makes the Wiener Vorlesungen so special is the close network of friendly ties that the city has been establishing with a growing circle of important academics and researchers. The speakers have come from all continents, countries and regions of the world. By inviting renowned academics, the City of Vienna has managed to ensure that it continually forms part of the global "scientific community". When planning and coordinating the Wiener Vorlesungen, particular care has always been paid to establishing, developing and fostering these friendly contacts.

The Wiener Vorlesungen strive to raise awareness of the complexity, dissimilarity and – frequently – contradictory nature of what we experience as social, cultural and political reality. The analytical-interpretative approach of the Wiener Vorlesungen dampens emotions and lays the foundations for overcoming problems by civil and democratic means. By participating in the Wiener Vorlesungen, the audience helps to "spread the virus" that is responsible for ensuring a good political climate.

Fernand Braudel described three totally different time levels of history, which were distinguished by their span and dynamics: 'L'histoire naturelle' encompasses the events that followed the rhythm and changes in nature, with a very long span and generally flat progress curves. 'L'histoire sociale' encompasses the social structures and developments, mentalities, symbols, and gestures. Compared with a human lifespan, these developments take much longer; in terms of our understanding of time, they have a "longue durée". And finally, he sees 'l'histoire événementielle' as the area of rapidly changing superficial events in political life.

Bearing these different conditions and time horizons of the present in mind, the Wiener Vorlesungen analyze the key problems that we will face in the future if we do not overcome them today. We are aware that human reality consists of material and discursive elements that are linked together through reciprocal relationships. The Wiener Vorlesungen broach the issue of contemporary relationship as facts and discourses. They analyze, evaluate and summarize them, facilitate the formation of opinions, and provide stimulus for further discussions.

Speakers to date include Marie Albu-Jahoda, Kofi Annan, Aleida Assmann, Jan Assmann, Jean Baudrillard, Ulrich Beck, Hans Belting, Bruno Bettelheim, Leon Botstein, Pierre Bourdieu, Christina von Braun, Elisabeth Bronfen, Ernesto Cardenal, Luc Ciompi, Carl Djerassi, Marion Dönhoff, Barbara Duden, Irenäus Eibl-Eibesfeldt, Manfred Eigen, Mario Erdheim, Amitai Etzioni, Valie Export, Vilem Flusser, Heinz von Foerster, Viktor Frankl, Peter Gay, Ute Gerhard, Maurice Godelier, Ernst Gombrich, Michail Gorbatschow, Marianne Gronemeyer, Karin Hausen, Jeanne Hersch, Eric J. Hobsbawm, Werner Hofmann, Ivan Illich, Eric Kandel, Verena Kast, Otto F. Kernberg, Rudolf Kirchschläger, Václav Klaus, Ruth Klüger, Teddy Kollek, Kardinal Franz König, György Konrad, Bischof Erwin Kräutler, Bruno Kreisky, Peter Kubelka, Hermann Lübbe, Niklas Luhmann, Viktor Matejka, Dennis L. Meadows, Adam Michnik, Hans Mommsen, Josef Penninger, Roger Penrose, Max F. Perutz, Hugo Portisch, Uta Ranke-Heinemann, Eva Reich, Marcel Reich-Ranicki, Horst-Eberhard Richter, Jeremy Rifkin, Erwin Ringel, Carl Schorske, Richard Sennett, Edward Shorter, Dorothee Sölle, Aminata Traoré, Marcel Tshiamalenga Ntumba, Desmond Tutu, Paul Watzlawick, Georg Weidenfeld, Erika Weinzierl, Ruth Wodak, Anton Zeilinger, Hans Zeisel, Jean Ziegler.

Peter Landesmann is a "permanent fellow" of the Wiener Vorlesungen. He has been involved in the project for many years, and has enhanced his expertise in the fields of Judaism, protestant and catholic theology, and comparative religious-scientific perspective during that time. In my function as editor of the series "Wiener Vorlesungen. Research", I am delighted that the honorary professor at the Institute for Jewish Studies who holds a triple PhD has deepened and expanded his thoughts first published in "The Birth of Christianity from Jewish Origins" by Picus Verlag in this publication.

Hubert Christian Ehalt

Contents

1. Preface

1.1. Introduction

Christianity perceives itself as the legacy of Judaism. The books of the Hebrew Bible were included in the Christian Bible as the "Old Testament". This integration extended even to the inclusion of 212 passages from the Hebrew Bible in the New Testament, some of which comprised several verses and some which were actually quoted several times over. As such, the Hebrew Bible became part of the Christian Bible, in the form of the "Old Testament".

Marcion (85 - 144 AD) was a theologian, who was later branded a heretic and who wanted to drive a wedge between the Hebrew Bible and the Gospels.

He believed that the Old Testament should be rejected since it proclaimed an angry, just and ultimately »evil« god (the God of Creation, the Demiurge), who had nothing in common with the God of Love who was exulted in the New Testament. Christ, who proclaimed this God of Love, had freed himself from the power of the Demiurge through his suffering in an illusory corporeal form (Docetism). This belief that the Jewish God was a vengeful, evil deity was subsequently expounded repeatedly, although the Church always discouraged such teachings.

If we strive to identify the difference between Christian religious belief and Judaism, it can be found in the contradictory perception of the person of Jesus. The issue that marked the beginning of the parting of the ways was the messianity of Jesus. We need to analyze the differing trends in Judaism that spawned the belief that God had sent a Redeemer in the person of the Messiah if we are to understand the origins of the term.

In the centuries leading up to the appearance of Jesus, Judaism was split into different groups, the best known of which were the Pharisees, the Sadducees and the Essenes. Beliefs differed, however, even among these groups themselves.

These diverse trends of thought emerged primarily as a result of the religious-philosophical, partly even mystical, trends from the Orient and Egypt, classical Greek philosophy, Persian culture and Hellenism that significantly influenced the Middle East region in the centuries leading up to the turning point in history.

Among the numerous trends of thought within Judaism, only those shall be mentioned that played a decisive role in molding Christianity. Although the beliefs examined below emerged one after the other, this does not mean that the earlier trends were superseded by their later counterparts. This diversity originated from the continued coexistence of the various religious beliefs alongside each other and from their assertion that they influenced, firstly the shaping of Judaism, and ultimately of Christianity.

This examination of the developments within Judaism that ultimately spawned Christianity will close by addressing the factor that played the most significant role in molding Christian anti-Judaism, which was the inner-Christian controversy between the Gentiles and the Jewish Christians. The accusations that Jewish Christians still practiced Jewish customs and therefore were not real Christians culminated in anti-Jewish writings, first by the fathers of the church and subsequently by other Christian theologians.

Diligent readers will detect many a contradiction in some of the Bible quotes. In many cases, these contradictions were bridged by exegeses of the text that can be found in a number of written works containing explanations of the Bible. Many of these were compiled into books called "Midrashim". (Singular: Midrash, the Hebrew word for interpretation.)

In the event that such a resolution of contradictions does not prove satisfactory, then the Rabbi saying prevails: "These and those are the words of the living God", which means that mankind's powers of comprehension are limited which is why it can find no explanations for what is only seemingly contradictory.

Both Jews and Christians adopted several different methods in their attempts to fathom the meaning of the Scriptures.

1.2 Multiple exegesis

1.2.1 The Jewish exegesis

The four most common approaches to exegesis originated in the Middle Ages and were summed up by the acronym "Pardes" (Paradise):

- The first consonant P stands for Pschat, the simple, literal meaning.
- The second consonant R stands for Remes, the symbolic or allegoric meaning.
- The third consonant D stands for Drasch: the interpretative, homiletic meaning.
- The last consonant S stands for Sod, which means secret and contains mystical, in many cases esoteric meanings. They should not be studied until the first three levels have been examined and understood.

These four approaches to exegesis are joined by the seven rules of Hillel (c. 30 BC - 9 AD) and the 13 rules of Rabbi Ishmael ben Elisha (90-135 AD), which are commonly cited, especially in the Talmud.

1.2.2 The Christian exegesis

Peter hints at the necessity for appropriate exegesis in his 2nd epistle: "...regard the patience of our Lord as salvation. So also our beloved brother Paul wrote to you according to the wisdom given him, speaking of this as he does in all his letters. There are some things in them hard to understand, which the ignorant and unstable twist to their own destruction, as they do the other scriptures" (2Pe 3:15-16 NRS).

John Cassian (around 360 - 435 AD) developed the method of four-step exegesis, which prevailed throughout the entire Middle Ages, based on the three-step exegesis devised by Origen. Similar to the Jewish tradition of bible exegesis (see PaRDeS), the historical-literal form of exegesis was then joined by three steps based on the principle of Faith-Love-Hope.

Literal meaning (literal, historical interpretation)
Allegorical meaning (interpretation based on "faith") = dogmatic
Tropological meaning (interpretation based on "love") = moral
Anagogical meaning (interpretation based on "hope") = apocalyptic

This raised the issue of ambiguity in the Scriptures, which then became the focus of reform efforts aimed at ensuring unambiguous exegeses.

In keeping with the newly rediscovered sense of historical awareness that emerged with the Renaissance, reformists rejected the four-step approach to exegesis. They wanted to get "to the source" (ad fontes) in historical (and theological) terms. They were solely interested in the literal meaning (sola scriptura).[1]

2. Mary's virgin birth as an introduction to biblical exegesis

Similar to the initial trial dig that is usually performed on archaeological digs, let us start by examining a controversial chapter, which can then be used as a basis for demonstrating the methodology and problems involved in bible exegesis.

To this end, some narratives of Mary's virgin birth are quoted below. They serve as examples to demonstrate the difficulties involved in analyzing text, while at the same time showing how statements can be couched in terms that are acceptable for believers although they are realistically void of reason.

"Now the birth of Jesus the Messiah took place in this way. When his mother Mary had been engaged to Joseph, but before they lived together, she was found to be with child from the Holy Spirit. Her husband Joseph, being a righteous man and unwilling to expose her to public disgrace, planned to dismiss her quietly. But just when he had resolved to do this, an angel of the Lord appeared to him in a dream and said, "Joseph, son of David, do not be afraid to take Mary as your wife, for the child conceived in her is from the Holy Spirit. She will bear a son, and you are to name him Jesus, for he will save his people from their sins." All this took place to fulfill what had been spoken by the Lord through the prophet: "Look, the virgin shall conceive and bear a son, and they shall name him Emmanuel," which means, "God is with us" (Mat 1:18-23 NRS).

The text is derived from Isa 7:14, which says:

"Therefore the Lord himself will give you a sign. Look, the young woman is with child and shall bear a son, and shall name him Immanuel" (Isa 7:14-16 NRS).

Instead of using "בְּתוּלָה", the word for virgin, the Hebrew text uses "עַלְמֹה" meaning "young woman". This distinction is ignored in the standard translation because the text was quoted according to the Septuagint, the Greek translation of the Hebrew Bible, where the term "παρθένος" (virgin) is used.

It is difficult to derive the origins of this translation which distorts the Hebrew text, although several different explanations have been attempted:

1. The translation was corrected retroactively by Christian writers. This claim could be plausible, given that – to this day – no pre-Christian written version of the Septuagint containing this section has ever been found.

6

2. Some academics claim that there would have been no clear distinction between the use of the words "בְּתוּלָה" and "עַלְמָה". This explanation is not accepted by Hebraists.
3. The person was translating the Septuagint from a different version of the Hebrew Bible where the term "בְּתוּלָה" was used in this passage. In actual fact, the text of the Hebrew Bible was indeed not standardized until post-Christian times. Before then, versions had been in circulation with albeit marginal, but nevertheless differing content. These findings were partially gleaned from an analysis of the scrolls found close by the Dead Sea.

Paul does not seem to know anything about the virgin birth as part of the new faith, as he writes:

"But when the fullness of time had come, God sent his Son, born of a woman, (ἐκ γυναικός) born under the law" (Gal 4:4 NRS). As such, he emphasizes the human birth, although he probably would have spotlighted the virgin birth if he had known about, and agreed with it.

Ignatius of Antioch, who died a martyr's death in the late years of Trajan's rule (Roman Emperor 98 - 117 AD), wrote to the Ephesians, 18:2: "For our God, Jesus the Christ, was conceived by Mary, in God's plan being sprung both from the seed of David and from the Holy Spirit." He thus harmonizes Jesus' lineage, citing Joseph, his father, as a descendant of King David, as can be derived from passages Mat 1:16 and Luk 1:27.

Augustine of Hippo, 354 - 430 AD, also found a passage in the Hebrew Bible to prove that both Jesus and Mary were conceived immaculately. He makes reference to Psalm 22:7: "But I am a worm and not a man, scorned by men and despised by the people." The birth of both Mary and Jesus was like that of worms, with no sex involved. (CChr 38,125).

An opinion voiced by Guibert of Nogent (1053 – 1124 AD) is characteristic of the anti-Judaic sentiment that prevailed in the late Middle Ages. He wrote a work entitled "De virginate opusculum" around 1120, in which he claims that Jews do not distinguish between Mary and other women. The sexual organs are healed when sexual lust, and therefore sin, is absent. Adam and Eve, cats, vultures, bees; they all show that reproduction is possible without the need for a sexual act. Jews only interpret the scripture literally because they are, by nature, attuned to matters of the flesh and are therefore akin to animals.

The Nicene Creed introduced by the first Council of Nicaea in 325 AD already mentions the Virgin Mary. The decisions adopted by the Council, which interpreted the text of the New Testament, are perceived to result from the influence of the Holy Spirit and, as such, believers can even accept so-called "miracles" as reality.

The Jewish scriptures also contain contradictions and reports of miracles which are not compatible with our inherent sense of rationalism. The Rabbinic school of thought was not trying to develop a theological doctrine; it wanted to draft a set of rules to govern "correct" behavior.

Jewish objections quoted by John the Evangelist prove that doubts about the immaculate conception were rife even back in Jesus' day: "They said to him: "We are not illegitimate children; we have one father, God himself" (Joh 8:41 NRS).

Mar 6:3 offers further arguments to contest Mary's virginity: "Is not this the carpenter, the son of Mary and brother of James and Joseph and Judas and Simon, and are not his sisters here with us?" (Mar 6:3 NRS). To counter this argument, the terms "brother" and "sister" are claimed to mean "cousin" as well. The wording "James the Lord's brother" in the letter Gal 1:19b. is also interpreted in this context (Gal 1:19 NRS).

In closing this chapter, it remains to be mentioned that the concept of the virgin birth aims to legitimize the origins of God.

Philo, an Alexandrian-Jewish philosopher (15/10 BC - 40 AD) elevates virginity to a higher level. One of his works (post 134) states: "XL. (134) Now of the four virtues, some are always virgins, and some from having been women become changed into virgins, as Sarah did; "For it had ceased to be with her after the manner of Women," (Genesis 18:11) when she began to conceive her happy offspring Isaac. But that which is always a virgin, is that of which Moses says, "And no man whatever knows her" (Gen 24:16). For in truth, it is not permitted to any mortal to pollute incorruptible nature, nor even clearly to comprehend what it is."

3. The Holy Spirit

The Holy Spirit is mentioned in Mt 1:18 as having been instrumental in the pregnancy of Mary: "Now the birth of Jesus the Messiah took place in this way. When his mother Mary had been engaged to Joseph, but before they lived together, she was found to be with child from the Holy Spirit." (Mat 1:18 NRS). The term "Holy Spirit" is mentioned several times in the Hebrew Bible. The following examples show that the "Holy Spirit" is responsible for inspiration from God:

"But they rebelled and grieved his holy spirit; therefore he became their enemy; he himself fought against them. Then they remembered the days of old, of Moses his servant. Where is the one who brought them up out of the sea with the shepherds of his flock? Where is the one who put within them his holy spirit" (Isa 63:10-11 NRS).

The Hebrew term "Ruach HaKodesch" which appears several times in Rabbi writings, is used both in this passage and in the following Psalm verse: "Do not cast me away from your presence, and do not take your holy spirit from me" (Psa 51:11 NRS). The expression "divine spirit" is used in the following quotes; an expression that equally signifies "divine inspiration":

"See, I have called by name Bezalel son of Uri son of Hur, of the tribe of Judah, and I have filled him with **divine spirit**, with ability, intelligence, and knowledge in every kind of craft" (Exo 31:2-3 NRS).

As the following sentence shows, even Gentiles can be touched by the "divine spirit":

"Balaam looked up and saw Israel camping tribe by tribe. Then the spirit of God came upon him" (Num 24:2 NRS).

The Acts of the Apostles (10:45) describes how Jews could not believe that the gift of the Holy Spirit was even given to Gentiles. In the following quotes, the expression "divine spirit" is combined with YHWH in Hebrew, whereas "El" or "Elohim" were the terms otherwise used in this expression: "The spirit of the Lord GOD is upon me, because the LORD has anointed me" (Isa 61:1 NRS). Equally: "The spirit of the LORD rushed on him" ("him" is Samson) (Jdg 14:6 NRS).

Philo also mentions the divine spirit, attributing the power of prophetic announcements to it:

"for a prophet does not utter anything whatever of his own, but is only an interpreter, another Being suggesting to him all that he utters, while he is speaking under inspiration, being in ignorance that his own reasoning powers are departed, and have quitted the citadel of his soul; while the divine spirit has entered in and taken up its abode there, and is operating upon all the organization of his voice, and making it sound to the distinct manifestation of all the prophecies which he is delivering" (spec 4, 49).

The following remark by Philo leads to the conclusion that the divine spirit whiled among the just for a long time:

"He...shall desist from doing wrong. In order that the divine spirit of wisdom may not be inclined to quit our neighborhood and depart, but that it may remain a very long time with us, as it did also with the wise Moses" (gig XI.47).

An analogy to this can be found in the Book of Wisdom (probably written between the 2nd century BC and 50 AD):

"For a holy and disciplined spirit will flee from deceit, and will leave foolish thoughts behind, and will be ashamed at the approach of unrighteousness" (Wis 1:5 NRS.)

In 381 AD, the First Council of Constantinople resolved that the Holy Spirit was also "truly God", i.e. the third person of the divinity. The Niceno-Constantinopolitan Creed includes the following decree:

"We believe in the Holy Spirit, the Lord, the giver of life, who proceeds from the Father (and the Son). With the Father and the Son he is worshipped and glorified. He has spoken through the Prophets."

The expression "and the son" is in brackets because the Eastern church claims that the Holy Spirit proceeds only from the Father.

4. Israel's hopes for the future

In most passages in the NT, Jesus is seen as the Messiah and numerous references imply his godlike nature.

As such, the origins of the Jewish belief in the Messiah need to first be examined.

Israel's political history is littered with numerous wars, most of which ended in defeat, and with just brief periods of peace between these wars. This situation repeatedly raised questions about the future of this country, which is small in terms of both population and land area. Over the course of time, the belief was fostered among the religious leaders of the people that the almighty and unique God of Israel would save his people and secure the eternal peace that they longed for so much. This level of deism is termed henotheism, which means that each ethnic community worshipped its God, just as Israel did.[2] This can also be found in numerous passages in the early books of the Bible.

For example: "You shall not bow down to them (other gods) or worship them; for I the LORD your God am a jealous God" (Exo 20:5 NRS), or "the LORD alone guided him; (Jacob) no foreign god was with him" (Deu 32:12 NRS). The sayings of the prophet Micah in the early 8th century BC also reveal that other nations worshipped other deities: "For all the peoples walk, each in the name of its god, but we will walk in the name of the LORD our God forever and ever" (Mic 4:5 NRS).

This God may have been omnipresent, but he was seated above the ark of the covenant, both in the sanctuary of the desert and in the Temple of Jerusalem. It was not until this Temple was destroyed by the Babylonians in 587 BC and the upper class Hebrews were exiled to Babylon that a truly monotheistic belief emerged in the writings of the prophets. Promulgating this belief among the people was not easy. Simple Israelites found it easier to grasp the concept of divine adoration that prevailed in their environment, i.e. worshipping "Baal", the "queen of heaven" and "idols" rather than some almighty, but invisible God. Even when in exile in Babylon, the people still worshipped their goddesses who were affiliated to the idols, such as "Asherah".

Anthropomorphist expressions describing God as a person are used in the Bible (e.g. the face of God in Gen 33:10 or the hand of God (Exo 33:22) and so on), which was partly due to the influence of Greek philosophy. As such, an attempt was made to align the invisible God with these expressions in the Bible. This was achieved through allegorical interpretation of the Bible, such as can be read in the works written by Philo.

It was the following sentence, above all, that formed the focus of religious dispute: "Then God said, "Let us make humankind in our image, according to our likeness" (Gen 1:26 NRS). Religious people, who might have been receptive to philosophical ideas, were upset by this sentence as it raised the question of whom these words were spoken to. The Jews opined they were angels, whereas the Christians use this sentence as proof of a trinity.

Philo also addressed this problem, drawing on Gen 3:22 "Behold, Adam has become as one of us, to know good and evil?" (Gen 3:22). The expression, "one of us" indicates a plurality of beings; unless indeed we are to suppose, that God is conversing with his own virtues, which he employed as instruments, as it were, to create the universe and all that is in it; but that expression "as" resembles an enigma, and a similitude, and a comparison, but is not declaratory of any dissimilarity; for that which is intelligible and sensibly good, and likewise that which is of a contrary character, is known to God in a different manner from that in which it is known to man; since, in the same way in which the natures of those who inquire and those who comprehend, and the things themselves too which are inquired into, and perceived, and comprehended, are distinguished, virtue itself is also capable of comprehending them. But all these things are similitudes, and forms, and images, among men; but among the gods they are prototypes, models, indications, and more manifest examples of things which are somewhat obscure; but the unborn and uncreated Father joins himself to no one, except with the intention of extending the honor of his virtues. (QG I,54).

The remoteness of God seems to have presented a further problem for monotheism, which was particularly characterized by the apocalypse, which will be examined later on. The remoteness of a transcendental, invisible God prompted some people to revert to the deities they had worshipped before. They probably asked themselves whether their prayers could reach this remote God and whether this God really cared about what was happening in the world.

Agents of God, whose job was to look after the people, were one means of abating this fear of having been deserted by God. Neither Judaism nor Christianity ever resolved this dichotomy between monotheism with "one single God" and a "royal household" of God where angels were God's servants.

By contrast, the people of Israel repeatedly suffered periods of deprivation and misery in their history. The term "God of Israel" was crucial to alleviate the feelings of hopelessness and demoralization and to inspire confidence in the future well-being of the people. This is why various homages to God have been handed down through the various époques in Israel's history that attribute the savior of the people wholly and solely to their God who is willing to fight for them:

"Happy are you, O Israel! Who is like you, a people saved by the LORD, the shield of your help, and the sword of your triumph! "Your enemies shall come fawning to you, and you shall tread on their backs" (Deu 33:29 NRS).

Equally:

"Say to those who are of a fearful heart, "Be strong, do not fear! Here is your God. He will come with vengeance, with terrible recompense. He will come and save you. Then the eyes of the blind shall be opened, and the ears of the deaf unstopped; then the lame shall leap like a deer, and the tongue of the speechless sing for joy. For waters shall break forth in the wilderness, and streams in the desert; the burning sand shall become a pool, and the thirsty ground springs of water; the haunt of jackals shall become a swamp, the grass shall become reeds and rushes" (Isa 35:4-7 NRS).

This prophetic saying actually links the rescue of Israel with a wondrous future that will even change nature.

"The spirit of the Lord GOD is upon me, because the LORD has anointed me; he has sent me to bring good news to the oppressed, to bind up the brokenhearted, to proclaim liberty to the captives, and release to the prisoners; to proclaim the year of the LORD's favor, and the day of vengeance of our God; to comfort all who mourn; to provide for those who mourn in Zion – to give them a garland instead of ashes, the oil of gladness instead of mourning, the mantle of praise instead of a faint spirit. They will be called oaks of righteousness, the planting of the LORD, to display his glory" (Isa 61:1-3 NRS).

Here, anointing (maschach) by God is used to allegorically represent the powers endowed on the prophet Isaiah. As such, the words he proclaims are the words of God. He is not acting as the Messiah; he is just prophesying what is to come, what will happen as a result of God's intervention. There is no further mention of any intervention by God against the enemies of Israel.

5. The Deuteronomic historical book

God personally took action, above all, in the Deuteronomic historical book, which comprises the Books of Deuteronomy, Joshua, Judges, 1 Samuel and 2 Samuel, and 1 Kings and 2 Kings, along with certain passages from the Book of Genesis.

The aforementioned books, which were edited by the "Deuteronomist"[3] and which rarely mention angels, probably reflect a degree of rationalization, e.g. the sacred temple is the place wherein the name of God dwells (Deu 12:5.11. and 21) but not God himself (1 Kin 8:13.). Furthermore, God spoke from his seat in heaven to Israel "out of the fire" (Deu 5:4 and 9 et seq, NRS) on the mountain, whereas this event is still described in the Book of Exodus as if God had come to Mount Sinai, where Moses had heard his voice (Exo 19). The ark was described in Deu 10:1et seqq merely as a container for the tablets containing the Ten Commandments, whereas it is still acknowledged as the "mercy seat" of God in Exo 25:22 (NRS) and 1Sam 4:4 (NRS).[4] Passages from Exo 23:20-33 are also quoted in Deu 6 and 7, albeit without the appearance of the angel who features prominently in the Book of Exodus. Everything is brought into being by the presence of God himself.[5]

6. The apocalyptic influence

The Book of Tobit emerged around 200 BC, containing the following prophesy: "But God will again have mercy on them, and God will bring them back into the land of Israel; and they will rebuild the temple of God, but not like the first one until the period when the times of fulfillment shall come. After this they all will return from their exile and will rebuild Jerusalem in splendor; and in it the temple of God will be rebuilt, just as the prophets of Israel have said concerning it" (Tob 14:5 NRS).

This passage addresses an issue that has featured repeatedly in prophetic predictions since 722 BC when the Assyrians conquered the northern kingdom and forced the population to relocate in other countries: The return of the descendants of these refugees to Israel.

The return of the displaced residents of the northern kingdom – whose location was not known even then and who were probably totally integrated into their new environment – was an unrealistic wish that only God could have granted since only He would have been able to find these refugees. Both this plea to God and the deliverance from the recurring acts of fate demanded intervention by a higher power. One of the outcomes of this wish, which could only be granted by a miracle, was the Apocalypse (Greek: αποκάλυψις, "unveiling", "revelation").

The influence of the Apocalypse on the region can be seen as the reversal of the trend towards rationalization as outlined in the previous chapter. The mysticism that was evolving in the Orient and Egypt also gradually started to influence the Jewish religion. This culminated in the apocalyptic scriptures in the second and first centuries BC, of which the Book of Enoch stands out in particular.

The "Day of the LORD" is even found in the writings of the prophet Amos dating back to the 8th century BC, which were edited in the 4th-5th century BC. Amos' prophecy of future events is structured as follows: First, the Israelites will be castigated for their behavior and required to repent, then will come the Day of the Lord, a Day of Judgment accompanied by a cosmic happening that only the "just" will survive, and they will then be promised a future in paradise:

"Hate evil and love good, and establish justice in the gate; it may be that the LORD, the God of hosts, will be gracious to the remnant of Joseph" (Amo 5:15 NRS). "Is not the day of the LORD darkness, not light, and gloom with no brightness in it?" (Amo 5:20 NRS). "I will restore the fortunes of my people Israel, and they shall rebuild the ruined cities and inhabit them; they shall plant vineyards and drink their wine, and they shall make gardens and eat their fruit. I will plant them upon their land, and they shall never again be plucked up out of the land that I have given them, says the LORD your God" (Amo 9:14-15 NRS).

The NT uses the expression "the day of our Lord Jesus Christ", in addition to "the day of the LORD": "just as the testimony of Christ has been strengthened among you – so that you are not lacking in any spiritual gift as you wait for the revealing of our Lord Jesus Christ. He will also strengthen you to the end, so that you may be blameless on the day of our Lord Jesus Christ" (1Cor 1:6-8 NRS) (1Cor 1:6 et seqq, similarly 1Cor 1:8; 2Cor 1:14; and "the day of God" in 2Pe 3:12 NRS and Acts 16:14 NRS).

Similar prophecies of an apocalyptic future to those voiced by the prophet Amos above can also be found in other parts of the Hebrew Bible, especially among the prophets Ezekiel, Isaiah and Joel.

This "day of the LORD" was equated with God's Day of Judgment, on which all the evil and, especially, the unbelievers would be punished and the just would be promised a pleasant continuation of their lives. The plight preceding this "day of the LORD" was later called the "labor of the Messiah". This expression, which features in Rabbi scriptures may have his origin from Isa 13:8 et seq: "and they will be dismayed. Pangs and agony will seize them; they will be in anguish like a woman in labor. They will look aghast at one another; their faces will be aflame. See, the day of the LORD comes, cruel, with wrath and fierce anger, to make the earth a desolation, and to destroy its sinners from it" (Isa 13:8-9 NRS).

Strictly speaking, the apocalyptic scriptures emerged after the 2nd century BC. They were written under pseudonyms: the actual author attributed his work to a well-known and respected biblical figure, who had lived centuries previously.

Enoch was an obvious front-line candidate for attribution of such an apocalyptic scripture since, according to the Bible, he did not die but was taken by God. Gen 5:24 describes the end of Enoch's life on earth as follows: "Enoch walked with God; then he was no more, because God took him" (Gen 5:24 NRS).

One characteristic feature of such apocalypses is the ascension to heaven with visions that are explained to the "chosen one" through an "interpret angel". Happenings in the past are represented as events that will occur in the future (vaticinium ex eventu). Usually, a day of final judgment for both the world and individual people is described. The adept is then brought back to earth and charged with keeping his knowledge of God's plan a secret or only disclosing it to a limited circle of people.

Mystic symbols of cosmic origin are described in great detail and then usually explained by the interpret angel. Another recurring feature of apocalyptic prophecies is the characteristics that distinguish God from Satan (good from evil) and this eon from the coming eon. (Isa 40 and 43 et seqq; Hag 2:15 -19; Zech 1:1-6).

The Apocalypse also exerted its influence on certain passages in the New Testament. This is why the "Revelation of John" in the New Testament is also rightly known as "John's Apocalypse".

The described ascension to heaven demonstrates how far God was removed from the world, a doctrine already related by Plato (428/427 BC - 348/347 BC) in his work Timaeus.

This remoteness of God is also perceivable in the Hebrew Bible: "Although heaven and the heaven of heavens belong to the LORD your God" (Deu 10:14 NRS).

The religious creative persons looked for agents of God who were sent by Him to the world and in whom they could trust in the hope that they would nevertheless not be exposed to the omnipresent dangers without some form of heavenly protection.

7. The titles given by God to agents acting on his behalf

7.1 The angels

The books of the Hebrew Bible also contain repeated mentions of angels, who were attributed to the sphere of God's power in Christian scriptures.

God's heavenly sphere was seen as a role model for the structures prevailing on earth from a relatively early stage, presumably between the 10th and 7th centuries BC. The sanctuary in the desert, for example, was based on what Moses saw on the Mount of Revelation. (Exo 26:30: Exo 27:8; Num 8:4.). Part of this image, whereby similar circumstances prevail on heaven as they do on earth, includes the idea that God has a "royal household", just like a King.

Angels are mentioned at fifteen verses of the Hebrew Bible. They are sent by God to earth with the power to perform deeds that should actually be reserved for God. The empowerment of the angels is particularly emphasized in the Second Book of Moses: "I am going to send an angel in front of you, to guard you on the way and to bring you to the place that I have prepared. Be attentive to him and listen to his voice; do not rebel against him, for he will not pardon your transgression; for my name is in him" (Exo 23:20-21 NRS).

During the 1st century BC or at the start of the 1st century AD, deliberations centered around angels embodying intermediate beings who were on God's staff, on the one hand, and the righteous who would live like angels in the world to come, on the other. Book 1 Enoch, for example, contains the following passage about angels: "In those days the mountains shall skip like rams, and the hills shall leap like young sheep satiated with milk; and all the righteous shall become like angels in heaven. Their countenance shall be bright with joy; for in those days shall the Elect One be exalted. The earth shall rejoice; the righteous shall inhabit it, and the elect possess it" (50:4 et seq)[6].

7.2 The Son of Man

The apocalyptic body of thought in the New Testament was combined with the personage of the Son of Man, for example in Mat 24,29: "Immediately after the suffering of those days the sun will be darkened, and the moon will not give its

18

light; the stars will fall from heaven, and the powers of heaven will be shaken. Then the sign of the **Son of Man** will appear in heaven, and then all the tribes of the earth will mourn, and they will see 'the Son of Man coming on the clouds of heaven' with power and great glory. And he will send out his **angels** with a loud trumpet call, and they will gather his elect from the four winds, from one end of heaven to the other" (Mat 24:29-31 NRS). (Similarly: Mar 13,24-27 NRS.)

In the Hebrew Bible, the term "Son of Man" first appears as "Ben Adam" in the Fourth Book of Moses (Num 23,19). It appears in similar form in Isa 51:12 and 56:2 and at 94 places in the Book of Ezekiel. The expression also features in the Psalms (Psa 8:5; 80:17; 146:3) with the exception of Psa 144:3 which cites: Ben-Anosch.

We first encounter the title "Son of Man" as a new term for a heavenly being empowered by God in the Book of Daniel. The Book of Daniel was assumed to be written around 160 BC.

We assume that Daniel's vision is dependent on that of Ezekiel:

"And above the dome over their heads there was something like a throne, in appearance like sapphire; and seated above the likeness of a throne was something that seemed like a human form" (Eze 1:26 NRS). Daniel turns the expression "like a human form" that Ezekiel uses into the title "Son of Man": "As I watched, thrones were set in place, and an Ancient One took his throne, his clothing was white as snow, and the hair of his head like pure wool; his throne was fiery flames, and its wheels were burning fire" (Dan 7:9 NRS). "As I watched in the night visions, I saw one **like a human being** coming with the clouds of heaven. And he came to the Ancient One and was presented before him. To him was given dominion and glory and kingship, that all peoples, nations, and languages should serve him. His dominion is an everlasting dominion that shall not pass away, and his kingship is one that shall never be destroyed" (Dan 7:13-14 NRS). A similar vision is described in 1 Enoch 46, 1-4:

"There I beheld the Ancient of days, whose head was like white wool, and with him another, whose countenance resembled that of man. His countenance was full of grace, like that of one of the holy angels. Then I inquired of one of the angels, who went with me, and who showed me every secret thing, concerning this **Son of man**; who he was; whence he was and why he accompanied the Ancient of days. He answered and said to me, This is the **Son of man**, to whom righteousness belongs; with whom righteousness has dwelt; and who will reveal all the treasures of that which is concealed: for the Lord of spirits has chosen him; and his portion has surpassed all before the Lord of spirits in everlasting uprightness. This **Son of man**, whom you behold, shall raise up kings and the mighty from their dwelling places, and the powerful from their thrones; shall loosen the bridles of the powerful, and break in pieces the teeth of sinners. He shall hurl kings from their thrones and their dominions; because they will not exalt and praise him, nor humble them selves before him, by whom their kingdoms were granted to them. The countenance likewise of the mighty shall He cast down, filling them with confusion. Darkness shall be their habitation, and worms shall be their bed; nor from that their bed shall they hope to be again raised, because they exalted not the name of the Lord of spirits."

1Enoch 46:1-4 sees the Son of Man as the "righteous one", similar to an **angel**, who was sent by God to strike down the powerful and the sinners who did not believe in Him.

Some of the quotes listed here resulted in the Messiah being seen as a Redeemer who would use force to assert his dominance. This notion of the Messiah then played a decisive role in the trial of Jesus and the decision to bring him before Pilate.

The return of the exiled tribes and the restoration of Israel's independence is no longer mentioned, unlike the later apocalyptic scriptures or the earlier prophecies, since Israel was already under the rule of the Jewish Hasmoneans from 164 BC onwards.

A further chapter from the First Book of Enoch, which probably dates from the end of the 1st century AD or even later (see end note 6), is particularly significant as that it sets the Son of Man on equal terms with the Messiah named in other Qumran scrolls. The Messiah is characterized, above all, by pre-existence and similarity to God:

1 Enoch 48, 2-5: "In that hour was this Son of man invoked before the Lord of spirits, and his name in the presence of the Ancient of days. Before the sun and the signs were created, before the stars of heaven were formed, his name was invoked in the presence of the Lord of spirits. A support shall he be for the righteous and the holy to lean upon, without falling; and he shall be the light of nations. He shall be the hope of those whose hearts are troubled. All, who dwell on earth, shall fall down and worship before him; shall bless and glorify him, and sing praises to the name of the Lord of spirits. Therefore the Elect and the Concealed One existed in his presence, before the world was created, and for ever."

Verse four of the same chapter does not clearly state, although the chosen wording certainly implies, that this Son of Man was revered – "shall fall down and worship before him" (proskynesis) – and that his glorification was equal to that of a second God, albeit diluted towards the end of the sentence – "and sing praises to the name of the Lord of spirits".

Paragraph 6 draws attention to the wisdom of God. This could be indicative of attempts to forge a connection between the doctrine of wisdom, which is yet to be described, and the doctrine of the Son of Man or Messiah.

The aforementioned proskynesis is described in the non-canonical Jewish Book of Sirach: "Then Simon came down and raised his hands over the whole congregation of Israelites, to pronounce the blessing of the Lord with his lips, and to glory in his name; and they bowed down in worship a second time, to receive the blessing from the Most High" (Sir 50:20-21 NRS). The mentioned "Simon" was the high priest Simon II (219 - 199 BC).

The Day of Judgment is also transferred to the Son of Man:

"He sat upon the throne of his glory; and the principal part of the judgment was assigned to him, the Son of man" (1 Enoch 68,39).

Similar prophecies to those about the Son of Man were also made about David and his descendants:

"Your house and your kingdom shall be made sure forever before me; your throne shall be established forever. In accordance with all these words and with all this vision, Nathan spoke to David" (2Sam 7:16-17 NRS).

The following quotation from 1 Enoch demonstrates an analogy to the prophecies about David's descendants: "the Elect One stands before the Lord of spirits; and his glory is for ever and ever; and his power from generation to generation" (1 Enoch 48a,2b).

So both his empowerment by God and his lineage as a descendant of David's tribe, Judah, were brought together in the Messianic doctrine.

This is why the listing of his ancestors, including King David, in Mat 1:6 is so important with respect to the Messianity of Jesus: "... and **Jesse the father of King David. And David was the father of Solomon** by the wife of Uriah, and Solomon the father of Rehoboam, and Rehoboam the father of Abijah, and Abijah the father of Asaph, and Asaph the father of Jehoshaphat, and Jehoshaphat the father of Joram, and Joram the father of Uzziah, and Uzziah the father of Jotham, and Jotham the father of Ahaz, and Ahaz the father of Hezekiah, and Hezekiah the father of Manasseh, and Manasseh the father of Amos, and Amos the father of Josiah, and Josiah the father of Jechoniah and his brothers, at the time of the deportation to Babylon. And after the deportation to Babylon: Jechoniah was the father of Salathiel, and Salathiel the father of Zerubbabel, and Zerubbabel the father of Abiud, and Abiud the father of Eliakim, and Eliakim the father of Azor, and Azor the father of Zadok, and Zadok the father of Achim, and Achim the father of Eliud, and Eliud the father of Eleazar, and Eleazar the father of Matthan, and Matthan the father of Jacob, **and Jacob the father of Joseph the husband of Mary, of whom Jesus was born, who is called the Messiah**" (Mat 1:6-16 NRS). Similarly: Luke 3:23-38 and Acts 13:22.

Jesus' ancestors are traced back through Joseph, his father. This cannot, however, be interpreted solely as a means of refuting the virgin birth of Jesus since

Roman law stipulated the patriarchal approach. No matter how a child becomes part of a family, it belongs to the kin of its father.

The next example shows that the doctrine of wisdom still continued to influence the hopes for the future that were linked to the "Son of Man":

"And in those days shall the Elect One sit upon his throne, while every secret of intellectual **wisdom** shall proceed from his mouth, for the Lord of spirits has gifted and glorified him" (Enoch 50:3).

7.3 The Messiah as a King and descendant of David

"King" is a further title that was first bestowed on God and later transferred to the Messiah.

The following quotations form part of the polemics that arose when the monarchy was introduced in Israel. Many people obviously perceived a monarchical form of government as a dismissal of the God of the Israelites. The following quotations emphasize that, although Israel expected to be ruled by a King again, it would continue to worship a God who is, himself, a King:

"The LORD will reign forever and ever" (Exo 15:18 NRS).

"... a king shall reign over us', though the LORD your God was your king" (1Sam 12:12b NRS).

"How beautiful upon the mountains are the feet of the messenger who announces peace, who brings good news, who announces salvation, who says to Zion, "Your God reigns" (Isa 52:7 NRS).

"the kingdom shall be the LORD's" (Oba 1:21NRS).

"The king of Israel, the LORD, is in your midst; you shall fear disaster no more" (Zep 3:15 NRS).

The saying in the 1st Book of Moses was also seen to imply the eternal rule of a King from the tribe of Judah: "The scepter shall not depart from Judah, nor the ruler's staff from between his feet, until tribute comes to him; and the obedience of the peoples is his" (Gen 49:10 NRS).

God's promise to David that the latter's descendants would rule Israel for eternity also had a long and significant knock-on effect. This passage also shows that the Divine Sonship initially referred to the King: "When your days are fulfilled and you lie down with your ancestors, I will raise up your offspring after you, who shall come forth from your body, and I will establish his kingdom. He shall build a house for my name, and I will establish the throne of his kingdom forever. I will be a father to him, and he shall be a son to me" (2Sam 07:12-14 NRS).

These words spoken by God prompted several prophets to predict that a descendant of David would be the redeemer of Israel and later the Messiah.

The following saying from the Psalms equally predicts the eternal existence of the kingdom but also emphasizes that this King will rule in a godlike, just manner, whereby Elohim is the word used for the title "God" in the Hebrew original. As we will see later, this title is a respectful glorification but does not express equality with God:

"Your throne, O God, endures forever and ever. Your royal scepter is a scepter of equity; you love righteousness and hate wickedness. Therefore God, your God, has anointed you with the oil of gladness beyond your companions" (Psa 45:6-7 NRS).

Both the aforementioned quotes and, in particular, the following quote from the Book of the Prophet Zechariah play a significant role in the interpretation of the self-perception of Jesus as Messiah and King, and will be examined in more detail later on:

"Rejoice greatly, O daughter Zion! Shout aloud, O daughter Jerusalem! Lo, your king comes to you; triumphant and victorious is he, humble and riding on a donkey, on a colt, the foal of a donkey" (Zec 9:9 NRS).

It is from this passage that the following quotation from the New Testament claims:

"Jesus found a young donkey and sat on it; as it is written: "Do not be afraid, daughter of Zion. Look, your king is coming, sitting on a donkey's colt!" (Joh 12:14-15 NRS). Similarly: Mat 21:2-7.

The Qumran scrolls predict that the future king will also free Israel, probably from Roman dominion:

"Chosen by God as scepter, who destroys by force and with the breath of his lips Israel's enemies" (1QSb = 1Q28b, Col 5,24). The following prophecy by Jeremiah indicates that the future Messianic ruler will proceed without force: "The days are surely coming, says the LORD, when I will raise up for David a righteous Branch, and he shall reign as king and deal wisely, and shall execute justice and righteousness in the land. In his days Judah will be saved and Israel will live in safety. And this is the name by which he will be called: "The LORD is our righteousness" (Jer 23:5-6 NRS).

As already mentioned, it was not just the apocryphal 1st Book of Enoch that played a decisive role in the emergence of the doctrine about the future Messiah, but also the bible, specifically in the prediction by the Prophet Micah:

"But you, O Bethlehem of Ephrathah, who are one of the little clans of Judah, from you shall come forth for me one who is to rule in Israel, whose origin is from of old, from ancient days" (Mic 5:2 NRS).

This passage reflects the view that the origins of the future ruler are extraterrestrial, since he came to the world before time began. This pre-existential origin was then transferred to the Messiah and is one of the reasons why Jesus was acknowledged as being on a par with God. .

A whole host of respectful names is bestowed on the coming ruler in Isa 9:6, including the title of God: "For a child has been born for us, a son given to us; authority rests upon his shoulders; and he is named Wonderful Counselor, Mighty God, Everlasting Father, Prince of Peace. His authority shall grow continually, and there shall be endless peace for the throne of David and his kingdom. He will establish and uphold it with justice and with righteousness from this time onward and forevermore. The zeal of the LORD of hosts will do this" (Isa 9:6-7 NRS).

Several passages in the Torah confer the respectful title of God (Hebr.: el or elohim, but never YHWH) on the Hebrew people or an extraordinary individual, and especially Moses, as demonstrated by the following quotes:

"I say, "You are gods, children of the Most High, all of you; nevertheless, you shall die like mortals, and fall like any prince" (Psa 82:6-7 NRS).

And:

"The LORD said to Moses, "See, I have made you like God to Pharaoh, and your brother Aaron shall be your prophet" (Exo 7:1 NRS). Similarly: Exo 4:16. Moses is also set apart by Ben Sira in the second century BC: "and was beloved by God and people, Moses, whose memory is blessed. He made him equal in glory to the holy ones, and made him great, to the terror of his enemies" (Sir 45:1-2 NRS). The word translated as "holy ones" is actually God in the Greek original text.

The title of Messiah for a Redeemer charged by God with saving Israel and mankind is only found in works written after the second century BC. Until then, two spiritual trends developed that contributed towards the shaping of the term "Messiah":

These are the doctrine of wisdom and the term "logos", which will be dealt with further on.

7.4 The Son of God

A further being predicted to be the savior of Israel is given the title "**Son of God**".

God imparts the following about his son and successor Salomon to King David in 2Sa 7:14: "I will be a father to him, and he shall be a son to me" (2Sa

7:14 NRS). This father-son relationship between God and the King is also illustrated by the "King psalms": "I will tell of the decree of the LORD: He said to me, "You are my son; today I have begotten you. Ask of me, and I will make the nations your heritage, and the ends of the earth your possession. You shall break them with a rod of iron, and dash them in pieces like a potter's vessel" (Psa 2:7-9 NRS). (Similarly: Psa 2:7 and Psa 28:9.)

This title "Son of GOD" is often bestowed on the Israelite people:

"When Israel was a child, I loved him, and out of Egypt I called my son" (Exo 11:1 NRS).

The Israelites are also described as Sons of God in Solomon's psalms, which were probably written in the 1st century BC: "And he shall not suffer unrighteousness to lodge any more in their midst, Nor shall there dwell with them any man that knoweth wickedness, For he shall know them, that they are all **sons of their God**" (PsS 17:29 et seq).

Proof that the title "Son of God" is a messianic title can be found in the Qumran scrolls: The title of Messiah is quoted together with the titles "Son of God" and "Son of the most high". (4Q 246, col 2, 1-7.).

8. The doctrine of wisdom and the term "logos"

The Jewish doctrine of wisdom first started emerging in the early years of Roman monarchy and was influenced by Oriental and Egyptian doctrines. This doctrine was then vastly enriched during the period of Hellenism. Even as far back as the 5th century BC, the leading religious figures among the Israelites are assumed to have become aware of the teachings of Greek philosophers.

The Greek word "philosophy" means "love of wisdom" and could have marked the starting point for the esteem in which wisdom is held. The verb "to philosophize" is first used by the Greek historian Herodotus (484 - 425 BC) (The Histories I,30,2). Heraclides Ponticus, a student of Plato who lived around 390 - 322 BC, passed down an account of Pythagoras apparently saying that only a God possessed true sophía, whereas "man" could only strive to achieve it. In this respect, sophia already refers to a metaphysical being. The credibility of this report by Heraclides, which has only been passed down indirectly and in fragments, is disputed among researchers. It is not until Plato, 428/427 - 348/347 BC, that the terms "philosophy" and "philosophies" are clearly used in the sense conveyed by Heraclides, and here especially in Plato's dialogue with Phaedrus (278d), where it is ascertained that anyone can strive for wisdom (philosophies) but only God is entitled to possess wisdom.

These Greek doctrines were adapted to the Jewish faith, and "wisdom" assumed a widespread significance in Jewish philosophy. The traditional stance adopted by Israel in respect of wisdom was founded on the basic assumption that the world was arranged in sensible order and ruled by YHWH, and that people were capable of recognizing this order. As such, wisdom is a characteristic of God that He bestows on people as well. It is not, however, an agent of God acting on its own initiative, unlike an angel, or the Messiah, the Son of God or the logos.

Paul reflects this view most accurately: "Ever since the creation of the world his eternal power and divine nature, invisible though they are, have been understood and seen through the things he has made" (Rom 1:20 NRS).

Justin the Martyr († around 165) writes in the same vein:

"We have been taught that Christ is the first-born of God, and we have declared above that He is the Word of whom every race of men were partakers; and those who lived reasonably are Christians, even though they have been thought atheists; as, among the Greeks, Socrates and Heraclitus, and men like them" (The First Apology 46).

In the early Books of the Hebrew Bible, wisdom is bestowed by God upon the people. e.g.: "And you shall speak to all who have ability, whom I have endowed with skill" (Exo 28:3 NRS). Or: "See, I have called by name Bezalel son of Uri son of Hur, of the tribe of Judah: and I have filled him with divine spirit, with ability, intelligence, and knowledge in every kind of craft" (Exo 31:2-3 NRS). During the period where the Deuteronomist Books were being written and/or edited – probably around the 6th century BC – wisdom was seen as a characteristic or a doctrine.

This is demonstrated by the following sentence, which shows that it was possible for a wise man, and not only God, to bestow wisdom on another person: "Joshua son of Nun was full of the spirit of wisdom, because Moses had laid his hands on him" (Deu 34:9 NRS). This sentence also served to credit Moses with godlike characteristics. It indicates a certain element of contradiction to Num 27:18, however, where it is stated that the spirit was already in Joshua before Moses laid his hands on him: "So the LORD said to Moses, "Take Joshua son of Nun, a man in whom is the spirit, and lay your hand upon him" (Num 27:18 NRS).

The Talmudic scholars defined a saying for exegesis in response to such contradictions, which occur frequently in the Hebrew Bible: "There is no earlier or later in the Torah" (bPes 6b;yShek VI,1 etc).

The First Books of both Kings and Chronicles show that the most outstanding characteristic of Solomon was his God-given wisdom. (For example: 1Ki 3:28).

The prophet Isaiah places "justice and righteousness" as well as "wisdom, and knowledge" on a par with "the fear of the LORD", but deems understanding of God's righteousness to be the highest virtue of mankind: "The LORD is exalted, he dwells on high; he filled Zion with justice and righteousness; he will be the stability of your times, abundance of salvation, wisdom, and knowledge; the fear of the LORD[7] is Zion's treasure" (Isa 33:5-6 NRS). Like the quotation by Isaiah above, the prophet Jeremiah, who lived in the first half of the 6th century, did not focus on the wisdom given to mankind: "Thus says the LORD: Do not let the wise boast in their wisdom, do not let the mighty boast in their might, do not let the wealthy boast in their wealth; but let those who boast in this, that they understand and know me, that I am the LORD; I act with steadfast love, justice, and righteousness in the earth, for in these things I delight, says the LORD" (Jer 9:23-24 NRS). As can be gleaned from the quotation above, the prophet Jeremiah may have qualified the wisdom of mankind and made it dependent on God, but he believed the wisdom of God to be one of His foremost characteris-

27

tics: "It is he who made the earth by his power, who established the world by his wisdom, and by his understanding stretched out the heavens" (Jer 51:15 NRS).

The prophet Ezekiel took a new stance on wisdom in 28:3-5 of his Book, which was possibly influenced by the emerging trend towards rationalism in Judaism, by understanding it as an attribute bestowed by nature on mankind that could not, however, be compared with the wisdom of God: "You (the prince of Tyre) are indeed wiser than Daniel; no secret is hidden from you; by your wisdom and your understanding you have amassed wealth for yourself, and have gathered gold and silver into your treasuries. By your great wisdom in trade you have increased your wealth, and your heart has become proud in your wealth. Therefore thus says the Lord GOD: Because you compare your mind with the mind of a god, therefore, I will bring strangers against you" (Eze 28:3-7a NRS).

The wisdom teaching is expressed as such in those biblical books that were written after the 5th century BC. One exception is the collection in the Book of Proverbs, which also contains older sayings, whereby the wisdom teachings in this Book were probably also written after the 5th century BC. The Wisdom Teachings include Job, Ecclesiastes, and the non-canonical Books of Sirach and Wisdom.

Most of the sayings explain the importance of wisdom in the lives of mankind. e.g.:

"And he said to humankind, 'Truly, the fear of the Lord, that is wisdom; and to depart from evil is understanding' (Job 28:28 NRS). As well as: 'Let the wise also hear and gain in learning, and the discerning acquire skill, ... The fear of the LORD is the beginning of knowledge; fools despise wisdom and instruction' (Pro 1:5-7 NRS). Equally: 'By me (the wisdom) kings reign, and rulers decree what is just; by me rulers rule, and nobles, all who govern rightly'" (Pro 8:15-16 NRS).

Two examples from Sirach: "Whoever fears the Lord will do this, and whoever holds to the law will obtain wisdom" (Sir 15:1 NRS). The following saying put wisdom on a par with the Torah: "Whoever obeys me will not be put to shame, and those who work with me will not sin. All this is the book of the covenant of the Most High God, the law that Moses commanded us as an inheritance for the congregations of Jacob" (Sir 24:22-23 NRS).

The following second sentence in 1 Enoch seems to have been added as it refers to the time after the destruction of the Temple in Jerusalem:

"Wisdom found not a place on earth where she could inhabit; her dwelling therefore is in heaven. Wisdom went forth to dwell among the sons of men, but she obtained not a habitation. Wisdom returned to her place, and seated herself in the midst of the angels. But iniquity went forth after her return, who unwillingly found a habitation, and resided among them, as rain in the desert, and as a dew in a thirsty land" (Chap.42,1 et seq).

28

The following final quotation on wisdom describes the connection between God and wisdom in the most vivid colors and sensitive poetry:
"For she (the wisdom) is a breath of the power of God, and a pure emanation of the glory of the Almighty; therefore nothing defiled gains entrance into her. For she is a reflection of eternal light, a spotless mirror of the working of God, and an image of his goodness" (Wis 7:25-26 NRS).

Academic opinions differ in respect of the nature of wisdom as depicted in the books of wisdom. Wisdom is personified in some passages and attributed with origins that date back to even before Creation, such as the Book of Proverbs 8:22-31:

"The LORD created me at the beginning of his work, the first of his acts of long ago. Ages ago I was set up, at the first, before the beginning of the earth. When there were no depths I was brought forth, when there were no springs abounding with water. Before the mountains had been shaped, before the hills, I was brought forth – when he had not yet made earth and fields, or the world's first bits of soil. When he established the heavens, I was there, when he drew a circle on the face of the deep, when he made firm the skies above, when he established the fountains of the deep, when he assigned to the sea its limit, so that the waters might not transgress his command, when he marked out the foundations of the earth, then I was beside him, like a master worker; and I was daily his delight, rejoicing before him always, rejoicing in his inhabited world and delighting in the human race" (Pro 8:22-31 NRS).

A similar approach is adopted in Sir 1:1-8: "All wisdom is from the Lord, and with him it remains forever. The sand of the sea, the drops of rain, and the days of eternity – who can count them? The height of heaven, the breadth of the earth, the abyss, and wisdom – who can search them out? Wisdom was created before all other things, and prudent understanding from eternity. The root of wisdom – to whom has it been revealed? Her subtleties – who knows them? There is but one who is wise, greatly to be feared, seated upon his throne – the Lord. It is he who created her; he saw her and took her measure; he poured her out upon all his works" (Sir 1:1-9 NRS).

Some see wisdom as the first of God's creations as a hypostasis of God, from which they derive the Holy Trinity of the Christian God. One argument against this opinion is that wisdom as an instrument of God is mainly meant to bring out the good in mankind and does not change the nature or fate of people or a nation, as shown by the following quotation:

"I, wisdom, live with prudence, and I attain knowledge and discretion. The fear of the LORD is hatred of evil. Pride and arrogance and the way of evil and perverted speech I hate. I have good advice and sound wisdom; I have insight, I have strength. By me kings reign, and rulers decree what is just; by me rulers rule, and nobles, all who govern rightly." (Pro 8:12-16 NRS).

The aforementioned quotation from Pro 8:22-31 is meant as a hymn in praise of wisdom and emphasizes that Creation reflects the wisdom of God, as can also be interpreted from the following sentence: "For she is an initiate in the knowledge of God, and an associate in his works" (Wis 8:4 NRS).

Unlike other beings begotten by God before Creation, wisdom does not intervene in events of the world. Pleading to God to bestow wisdom on a person would, moreover, not be possible if we were to assume it is a hypostasis of God. Such a plea appears in the Book of Wisdom: "give me the wisdom that sits by your throne, and do not reject me from among your servants" (Wis 9:4 NRS). In this case, wisdom is seen as a heavenly being that is seated next to God in heaven, like the angels. This does not, however, mean that wisdom is therefore seen as a second God or as a personification of God.

Philo also connected wisdom as a positive element and not a hypostasis with God and the world. For example, Philo contradicts teachings that see personified wisdom as any form of hypostasis of God. To this end, he writes: "human wisdom has two origins: one is divine, the other is natural" (her. 182). In his work "on Flight and Finding", fug. 52, he even gives his own description of wisdom, probably in an allegorical if not even ironic sense: "daughter of God, wisdom, that is, who, though a daughter, is also a father" (52). "...but not only is wisdom like light, the instrument of seeing, but it does also behold itself. This, in God, is the light which is the archetypal model of the sun, and the sun itself is only its image and copy; and he who shows each thing is the only all-knowing being, God; for men are called knowing only because they appear to know; but God, who really does know, is spoken of, as to his knowledge, in a manner inferior to its real nature, for everything that is ever spoken in his praise comes short of the real power of the living God. And he recommends his wisdom, not merely by the fact that it was he who created the world, but also by that of his having established the knowledge of everything that has happened, or that has been created in the firmest manner close to himself " (migr VIII. 40 et seq). "Moreover, wisdom is a thing not only more ancient than my own birth, but even than the creation of the universal world; nor is it lawful nor possible for any one to decide in such a matter but God alone, and those who love wisdom with guilelessness, and sincerity and truth" (virt, X,62).

The following sentences in the Book of Wisdom are important for assessing the perception of the status of wisdom in wisdom teachings: "O God of my ancestors and Lord of mercy, who have made all things by your word, and by your wisdom have formed humankind to have dominion over the creatures you have made" (Wis 9:1-2 NRS) and in Sirach: "The root of wisdom – to whom has it been revealed? Her subtleties – who knows them? There is but one who is wise, greatly to be feared, seated upon his throne – the Lord. It is he who created her; he saw her and took her measure; he poured her out upon all his works, upon all the living according to his gift; he lavished her upon those who love him" (Sir 1:6-10 NRS).

Around 300 BC, Zeno of Citium introduced the school of stoicism by devising the theory that the principle of commonality of all world phenomena could be identified by Reason. This principle, which he called logos, was a static origin from which all activities derived Logos means word and speech and sense and could therefore also symbolize God.

The Book of the prophet Isaiah represents the "Word of God" as an independent creation of God: "For as the rain and the snow come down from heaven, and do not return there until they have watered the earth, making it bring forth and sprout, giving seed to the sower and bread to the eater, so shall my word be that goes out from my mouth; it shall not return to me empty, but it shall accomplish that which I purpose, and succeed in the thing for which I sent it" (Isa 55:10-11 NRS).[8]

According to logos teaching, the divine logos emerges from God at Creation, as can be gleaned from John's prologue:

"In the beginning was the Word, and the Word was with God, and the Word was God. He was in the beginning with God. All things came into being through him, and without him not one thing came into being. What has come into being in him was life, and the life was the light of all people" (Joh 1:1-4 NRS).

These words are based on the history of Creation in the First Book of Moses, chapter 1, where it says: "God said" and, in saying so, the world was created.

The wisdom teachings were integrated into the logos teachings, so to speak, as described in the Book of Wisdom 9,1, as already mentioned above: "O God of my ancestors and Lord of mercy, who have made all things by your word" (Wis 9:1 NRS).

Philo claims: "Thus, therefore, putting all these things together, God appropriated the dominion over them all to himself, but the use and enjoyment of themselves and of each other he allowed to those who are subject to him; for we have the complete use of our own faculties and of everything which affects us: I therefore, consisting of soul and body, and appearing to have a mind (Wisdom), and reason (Logos), and outward sense, find that not one of all these things is my own property" (cher I, XXXII. (113).

The "Word of God", the logos that was directed at the prophets also first had to be understood by them, which is why "Hear the word of the LORD" (Isa 1:10 NRS), meaning receive the word of God is found in several places in the Hebrew Bible. The thought provoked by divine inspiration is then expressed in speech with the aim of defining people's behavior. In the sense of "loving the LORD your God, obeying him, and holding fast to him; for that means life to you and length of days" (Deu 30:20 NRS).

Philo of Alexandria called logos the Son of God and the mediator between God and mankind; he also saw him as the "epitome of all creative ideas".

The following deliberations by Philo of Alexandria, a Jewish-Hellenistic philosopher and theologian (*15-10 BC - after 40 AD), are important for the development of the Christian doctrine about the divinity of Jesus:

Philo raises the following thought: "Why does God say "for in his own image God made humankind" in Gen 9:6? "He answers the question thus: "What is the man who was created? And how is that man distinguished who was made after the image of God?" (Gen 2:7). "This man was created as perceptible to the senses, and in the similitude of a Being appreciable only by the intellect; but he who in respect of his form is intellectual and incorporeal, is the similitude of the **archetypal model** (second God) as to appearance, and he is the form of the principal character; but this is the word of God (logos), the first beginning of all things, the original species or the archetypal idea, the first measure of the universe" (QG I,4).

Philo adopts the same stance in his work "Who is the Heir of Divine Things": "And the Word (logos) rejoices in the gift, and, exulting in it, announces it and boasts of it, saying, "And I (logos) stood in the midst, between the Lord and You;" (Num 16:48.) neither being uncreate as God, nor yet created as you, but being in the midst between these two extremities, like a hostage, as it were, to both parties: a hostage to the Creator, as a pledge and security that the whole race would never fly off and revolt entirely, choosing disorder rather than order; and to the creature, to lead it to entertain a confident hope that the merciful God would not overlook his own work. For I will proclaim peaceful intelligence to the creation from him who has determined to destroy wars, namely God, who is ever the guardian of peace" (her, XLII, § 206).

Philo's interpretation of num 16:48 is characteristic of his allegorical interpretation of the bible. This verse refers to the outbreak of the plague, which Aaron cured, and reads as follows: "So Aaron took it as Moses had ordered, and ran into the middle of the assembly, where the plague had already begun among the people. He put on the incense, and made atonement for the people. **He stood between the dead and the living**; and the plague was stopped" (Num 16:47-48 NRS). Philo understood the word "he", describing Aaron, the first high priest, as the logos and the words **"dead and the living"** as mortals and immortals". Which is how he arrived at "mankind and God" using his allegorical method, and therefor he writes the following, as can be seen from the quotation above: "And I (logos) stood in the midst, between the Lord and You."

"Therefore the sacred Word, (logos) having given us instruction respecting the division into equal parts, leads us also to the knowledge of opposites, saying that God placed the divisions "**opposite to one Another**" (Gen 15:10) (her, XLIII. §207).

Philo took this quotation of the context of the following verse: "Bring me a heifer three years old, a female goat three years old, a ram three years old, a turtledove, and a young pigeon." He brought him all these and cut them in two, laying each half **over against the other**" (Gen 15:9-10 NRS).

Philo describes his notion of logos in more detail in his work "On Husbandry", whereby he also describes **angels** as a hypostasis of God: "For God, like a shepherd and a king, governs (as if they were a flock of sheep) the earth, and the water, and the air, and the fire, and all the plants, and living creatures that are in them, whether mortal or divine; and he regulates the nature of the heaven, and the periodical revolutions of the sun and moon, and the variations and harmonious movements of the other stars, ruling them according to law and justice; appointing, as their immediate **superintendent**, his own right reason (logos), his **first-born son**, who is to receive the charge of this sacred company, as the lieutenant of the great king; for it is said somewhere, "Behold, I am he! I will send my messenger (angel) before thy face, who shall keep thee in the Road" (Exo 23:20.) (Act XII. 51).

It would seem that Philo made this statement so as not to jeopardize the monotheist body of thought. This is possibly why he wrote the following clarification: "And the good man (combination of wisdom and logos) is on the borders, so that one may appropriately say that he is neither God nor man, but that he touches the extremities of both, being connected with the mortal race (wisdom) by his manhood, and with the immortal race (logos) by his virtue. And there is something which closely resembles this in the passage of scripture concerning the high priest; "For when," says the scripture, "he goes into the holy of holies, he will not be a man till he has gone out again" (Lev 16:17). But if at that time he is not a man, it is clear that he is not God either, but a minister of God, belonging as to his mortal nature to creation, but as to his immortal nature to the uncreated God. (somn. 2.230 et seq). Philo interprets the text of Lev 16:17: "No one shall be in the tent of meeting from the time he enters to make atonement in the shrine until he comes out and has made atonement for himself and for his house and for all the assembly of Israel" (Lev 16:17 NRS). Instead of "no one" he translates the Hebrew text as "no man" וְכָל־אָדָם לֹא־יִהְיֶה

9. The statements made by Jesus about Judaism

"One of the scribes came near and heard them disputing with one another, and seeing that he answered them well, he asked him, "Which commandment is the first of all?" Jesus answered, "The first is, 'Hear, O Israel: the Lord our God, the Lord is one; you shall love the Lord your God with all your heart, and with all your soul, and with all your mind, and with all your strength.' The second is this, 'You shall love your neighbor as yourself.' There is no other commandment greater than these." Then the scribe said to him, "You are right, Teacher; you have truly said that "he is one, and besides him there is no other" (Mar 12:28-32 NRS). The texts recited by Jesus are from the Torah, as follows: "Hear, O Israel: The LORD is our God, the LORD alone. You shall love the LORD your God with all your heart, and with all your soul, and with all your might" (Deu 6:4-5 NRS), and "you shall love your neighbor as yourself" (Lev 19:18 NRS).

In the following quotation from Matthew, Jesus mentions the Ten Commandments and the commandment of love as defined in the Torah (Deu 5:16.18 et seqq and Exo 20:12,14 et seqq), which assure longevity to the person who abides by them:

"Then someone came to him and said, "Teacher, what good deed must I do to have eternal life?" And he said to him, "Why do you ask me about what is good? There is only one who is good. If you wish to enter into life, keep the commandments." He said to him "Which ones?" And Jesus said, "You shall not murder; You shall not commit adultery; You shall not steal; You shall not bear false witness; Honor your father and mother; also, You shall love your neighbor as yourself" (Mat 19:16-19 NRS). Along the same lines, Jesus emphasizes that the foremost commandments can be found in the Torah and among the prophets:

It seems that Matthew placed the utmost importance on these laws, since he repeats those words in Mat 22,36-38. Here Matthew adds the following words of Jesus: "On these two commandments hang all the law and the prophets" (Mat 22:40 NRS).

Jesus saw it as his mission to convert the Jews to their laws, which he did not want to change, but wanted them interpreted humanely. As is shown by the following quotation:

"For truly I tell you, until heaven and earth pass away, not one letter, not one stroke of a letter, will pass from the law until all is accomplished" (Mat 5:18 NRS).

He gave his disciples the following instructions:

"These twelve Jesus sent out with the following instructions: "Go nowhere among the Gentiles, and enter no town of the Samaritans, but go rather to the lost sheep of the house of Israel" (Mat 10:5-6 NRS). (Similarly: Mat 16:24).

In the Sermon on the Mount (Mat 5,) Jesus propagates for a stricter application of the Commandment of Love. He probably took the following remark about hating enemies from apocalyptic statements, such as found in the Qumran scrolls, since no such Commandment features in the Hebrew Bible:

"You have heard that it was said, 'You shall love your neighbor and hate your enemy.' But I say to you, Love your enemies and pray for those who persecute you" (Mat 5:43-44 NRS).

The Hebrew Bible says the following about how people should behave towards their enemies: "If your enemies are hungry, give them bread to eat; and if they are thirsty, give them water to drink; for you will heap coals of fire on their heads, and the LORD will reward you" (Pro 25:21-22 NRS).

Jesus' interpretation of the Sabbath laws is further proof of his humane attitude:

"One man was there who had been ill for thirty-eight years. When Jesus saw him lying there and knew that he had been there a long time, he said to him, "Do you want to be made well?" The sick man answered him, "Sir, I have no one to put me into the pool when the water is stirred up; and while I am making my way, someone else steps down ahead of me."

Jesus said to him, "Stand up, take your mat and walk." At once the man was made well, and he took up his mat and began to walk. Now that day was a sabbath. So the Jews said to the man who had been cured, "It is the sabbath; it is not lawful for you to carry your mat" (Joh 5:5-10 NRS).

Equally:

"He (Jesus) left that place and entered their synagogue; a man was there with a withered hand, and they asked him, "Is it lawful to cure on the sabbath?" so that they might accuse him. He said to them, "Suppose one of you has only one sheep and it falls into a pit on the sabbath; will you not lay hold of it and lift it out? How much more valuable is a human being than a sheep! So it is lawful to do good on the sabbath" (Mat 12:9-12 NRS).[9]

The exegesis attributed to Jesus and the code of conduct he practiced are shared by all progressive Jews nowadays.

Next, we will examine the self-perception of Jesus. In doing so, we need to bear in mind that the earliest texts that have been passed down are the Letters of

Paul, which were probably written between 50 and 60 AD, so some twenty years after the Passion of Jesus. The Gospels are generally assumed to have been written between 70 and 90 AD. As such, there is no certain proof that the statements attributed to Jesus in the New Testament were actually made by him. This is, however, relatively unimportant in respect of the emergence of Christianity. What is important is which words were attributed to Jesus in the period following his crucifixion.

Jesus' attitude towards the Temple in Jerusalem is clear: He regularly visited the Temple to teach there (Mat 21:23; 26:55; Mar 12:35 et seqq, etc.). He was offended by the merchants doing business in a holy place and wanted to preserve the dignity of the Temple, which explains the following sentence:

"Then Jesus entered the temple and drove out all who were selling and buying in the temple, and he overturned the tables of the money changers and the seats of those who sold doves. He said to them, "It is written, My house shall be called a house of prayer; but you are making it a den of robbers" (Mat 21:12-13 NRS), similarly: (Mat 21:12f; Mar 11:15 et seqq).

Two statements attributed by the evangelists to Jesus are not commensurate with his image as a believing Jew. They are:

"For the Son of Man is lord of the sabbath" (Mat 12:8 NRS). Even if Jesus did see himself as the Messiah, the Messiah would not have had the power to change the law, as is also reflected in the statements attributed to Jesus, although the Torah, or at least parts of it, will be no longer applied in the Messianic period according to some Rabbinical texts. Just like the Rabbis before him, Jesus only reinterpreted the laws, applying a stricter interpretation of the rules that derived from tradition. As far as the first claim is concerned, we can refer to Mat 5:18: "For truly I tell you, until heaven and earth pass away, not one letter, not one stroke of a letter, will pass from the law until all is accomplished. Therefore, whoever breaks one of the least of these commandments, and teaches others to do the same, will be called least in the kingdom of heaven; but whoever does them and teaches them will be called great in the kingdom of heaven" (Mat 5:18-19 NRS).

As far as the second claim - tightening the laws - is concerned, reference is made to Mar 11:16: "he (Jesus) would not allow anyone to carry anything through the temple" (Mar 11:16 NRS).[10]

Whether the following sentence really reflected Jesus' attitude is equally doubtful: "since it enters, not the heart but the stomach, and goes out into the sewer?" (Thus he declared all foods clean) (Mar 7:19 NRS). This is indicative of the stance adopted by many Christian bible scholars who equally believe that the end of Mar 7:19 was added at a later date. This is why the translators parenthesized the passage in the New Revised Standard (NRS).[11]

Compliance with certain food rules didn't become an issue until Gentiles started being baptized but without having been commited to obeying Jewish laws.

The clearest statement about Jesus as a Jew can be found in words said by Jesus that were passed down by John the Evangelist: "for salvation is from the Jews" (Joh 4:22 NRS). This record is all the more credible since John the Evangelist also passed down words of Jesus that definitely can be termed anti-Jewish. e.g.: "You (his Jewish opponent) are from your father the devil" (Joh 8:44 NRS). As already mentioned, these words were not written down until about sixty years after Jesus' death and are therefore indicative of the perception that prevailed at the time of John writing his Gospel.

10. The titles bestowed on Jesus

All of the titles bestowed on Jesus in the New Testament have their origin in Judaism and show that, not only did Jesus feel that he was a Jew, but also the people in Palestine at the time also saw him as a Jew. This is evidenced by the following passages from the New Testament.

10.1 Jesus, the Rabbi and Teacher

"Now there was a Pharisee named Nicodemus, a leader of the Jews. He came to Jesus by night and said to him "Rabbi, we know that you are a teacher who has come from God; for no one can do these signs that you do apart from the presence of God" (Joh 3:1-2 NRS).

10.2 Jesus, the Prophet

It was not until the period of Rabbinic Judaism that the Book of "Malachi" was designated the last Book of the Prophets.[12] This is also indicated in 1 Maccabees 9:26 as follows: "So there was great distress in Israel, such as had not been since the time that prophets ceased to appear among them" (1Ma 9:27 NRS). Two passages in 1Ma do, however, indicate that the coming of a prophet was anticipated in the period following the 2nd century BC: "...and stored the stones in a convenient place on the temple hill until a prophet should come to tell what to do with them" (1Ma 4:46 NRS). "The Jews and their priests have resolved that Simon should be their leader and high priest forever, until a trustworthy prophet should arise" (1Ma 14:41 NRS).

Moses' prophesy in Deu 18,15 further contributed towards this anticipation: "The LORD your God will raise up for you a prophet like me from among your own people; you shall heed such a prophet" (Deu 18:15 NRS).

When addressing a congregation, Peter used this verse from the Torah as proof that Jesus is the prophet, whose coming had been foretold by Moses: "Moses said, "The Lord your God will raise up for you from your own people a prophet like me. You must listen to whatever he tells you. And it will be that everyone who does not listen to that prophet will be utterly rooted out of the people." And all the prophets, as many as have spoken, from Samuel and those after him, also predicted these days. You are the descendants of the prophets and of the covenant that God gave to your ancestors, saying to Abraham, "And in your descendants all the families of the earth shall be blessed" (Act 3:22-25 NRS).

This anticipation is probably the reason why many saw Jesus as a prophet because of his miracle healing powers and his obviously charismatic appearance: "The woman said to him, "Sir, I see that you are a prophet" (Joh 04:19 NRS). Equally: "... Jesus of Nazareth, who was a prophet mighty in deed and word before God and all the people" (Luk 24:19b NRS).

The widespread opinion that Jesus was a prophet is illustrated by the words used by the people to mock Jesus when he was brought before the High Priest: "Prophesy to us, you Messiah! Who is it that struck you?" (Mat 26:68 NRS) (similarly: Luk 22:64; Mar 14:65).

10.3 Jesus, the High Priest

This is another title that is bestowed on Jesus in the Letter to the Hebrews in the NT: "And one does not presume to take this honor, but takes it only when called by God, just as Aaron was. So also Christ did not glorify himself in becoming a high priest, but was appointed by the one who said to him, "You are my Son, today I have begotten you"; as he says also in another place, "You are a priest forever, according to the order of Melchizedek" (Heb 5:4-6 NRS).

A tradition emerged at the latest in the 1st century BC by which Melchizedek was judged to be a High Priest. Gen 14 narrates that Melchizedek was a King and Priest who blessed Abraham: "And King Melchizedek of Salem brought out bread and wine; he was priest of God Most High" (Gen 14:18 NRS). The High Priest is represented as superhuman in the passages about "Melchizedek" in the Qumran scrolls (11Qmelch or 11Q13) and the "Testament of Levi" (1st - 2nd century AD).

Psalm 110 describes words of God directed at David: "The LORD has sworn and will not change his mind, "You are a priest forever according to the order of Melchizedek" (Psa 110:4 NRS). This was the only means of justifying the designation of David as a priest since he was not from the priestly caste of the Levites, whose founder Levi was one of Jacob's sons. The High Priest always came from the caste of Aaron, the brother of Moses. As already mentioned, David was a descendant of Judah, who was also one of Jacob's sons. So Melchizedek – the founder of a dynasty of priests – was drawn upon in the bible verse quoted above in order to bestow the title of priest on David. These were also the grounds on which Jesus was designated a High Priest: "This was confirmed with an oath; for others who became priests took their office without an oath, but this one became a priest with an oath, because of the one who said to him "The Lord has sworn and will not change his mind, You are a priest forever" – accordingly Jesus has also become the guarantee of a better covenant. Furthermore, the former priests were many in number, because they were prevented by death from continuing in office; but he holds his priesthood permanently, because he continues forever. Consequently he is able for all time to save those who approach God through him, since he always lives to make intercession for them. For it was fitting that we should have such a high priest, holy, blameless, undefiled, separated from sinners, and exalted above the heavens. Unlike the other high priests, he has no need to offer sacrifices day after day, first for his own sins, and then for those of the people; this he did once for all when he offered himself" (Heb 7:20-27 NRS).

The reference at the end of the quotation above, whereby sacrifices became meaningless following Jesus' sacrifice, will be revisited in Chapter 29 when discussing the mosaics in the Theotokos Chapel and Church of Sts. Lot and Procopius on Mount Nebo and in the church on the acropolis at Main.

"Christ" is the title most commonly used for Jesus in the New Testament. "Christos" is Greek for "the anointed one". As already explained, anointment was a ritual for consecrating a King, although the Bible does not mention it for each new King.[13] The High Priest was also anointed although this is only occasionally reported in the Bible. Messiah is Hebrew, and Christos is Greek for "the anointed one". It is unlikely that the Greek word "Christos" would be used during Jesus' lifetime in the region of Palestine as the people spoke Aramaic.

10.4 Jesus, the King

The title of King for Jesus refers to his title of "Christ", since the consecration of a King in Israel included anointment. The mentioned prophecies about the advent of the Messiah are inseparably linked to the title of King for Jesus, who was a descendant of King David according to Matthew and and Luke.

The following statements made by Jesus will also be revisited in an attempt to resolve the question as to why Jesus was crucified:

"Pilate asked him, "So you are a king?" Jesus answered, "You say that I am a king. For this I was born, and for this I came into the world, to testify to the truth. Everyone who belongs to the truth listens to my voice" (Joh 18:37 NRS).

"Then Pilate asked him, "Are you the king of the Jews?" He answered, "You say so" (Luk 23:3 NRS). The Gospel according to Mark provides evidence that Jesus claimed the title of King for himself, or that it was claimed by his disciples, where both the Roman soldiers and the people mocked Jesus as King:

"Hail, King of the Jews!" (Mar 15:18 NRS). "Let the Messiah, the King of Israel, come down from the cross now, so that we may see and believe" (Mar 15:32 NRS).

The Gospel according to John also bears witness to the use of the title "King", which was unlawful in the eyes of the Romans: "Pilate also had an inscription written and put on the cross. It read "Jesus of Nazareth, the King of the Jews" (Joh 19:19 NRS).

The objection by the priests as reported by John the Evangelist also illustrates the likelihood that Pilate really did have the inscription made: "Then the chief priests of the Jews said to Pilate, "Do not write, "The King of the Jews" but, "This man said, I am King of the Jews" (Joh 19:21 NRS).

10.5 Jesus, the "Savior"

The texts in the New Testament do not always make it clear, how the title of "Savior" for Jesus should be interpreted. The Judaist perception of the Messiah as a savior was political, as illustrated in several quotations in the first part of this scripture; they saw him as the savior of Israel's national independence, a quality that the Hebrew Bible also attributes to the anticipated Redeemer: "Hear the word of the LORD, O nations, and declare it in the coastlands far away; say ,He who scattered Israel will gather him, and will keep him as a shepherd a flock. For the LORD has ransomed Jacob, and has redeemed him from hands too strong for him" (Jer 31:10-11 NRS).

"Their Redeemer is strong; the LORD of hosts is his name. He will surely plead their cause, that he may give rest to the earth, but unrest to the inhabitants of Babylon. A sword against the Chaldeans, says the LORD, and against the inhabitants of Babylon, and against her officials and her sages!" (Jer 50:34-35 NRS).

Some references show that the disciples of Jesus also expected this type of redemption from him: "But we had hoped that he was the one to redeem Israel" (Luk 24:21 NRS). "Blessed be the Lord God of Israel, for he has looked favorably on his people and redeemed them. He has raised up a mighty savior for us in the house of his servant David, as he spoke through the mouth of his holy prophets from of old, that we would be saved from our enemies and from the hand of all who hate us" (Luk 1:68-71 NRS).

Equally: "So when they had come together, they asked him "Lord, is this the time when you will restore the kingdom to Israel?" (Act 1:6 NRS). The following quotation links the redemption not to the restoration of Israel's sovereignty but to the savior from sin: "God exalted him at his right hand as Leader and Savior that he might give repentance to Israel and forgiveness of sins" (Act 5:31 NRS).

The interpretation of the word "Savior" is ambivalent in the following sentences: "to you is born this day in the city of David a Savior, who is the Messiah, the Lord" (Luk 2:11 NRS). "I have found David, son of Jesse, to be a man after my heart, who will carry out all my wishes. Of this man's posterity God has brought to Israel a Savior, Jesus, as he promised" (Act 13:22-23 NRS).

The following statement is more comprehensive and cannot be interpreted as political nor restricted to the forgiveness of sins. Its meaning is more metaphysical: "and we know that this is truly the Savior of the world" (Joh 4:42 NRS). The term "Savior" is linked to "Redemption". See chapters 18 and 19 in this respect.

10.6 "Lord" as a title for Jesus

The Hebrew Bible generally uses "Lord" as a description of "God", although the word is also used in its conventional sense in some places (e.g. Gen 39:19).

In the Septuagint, the Greek Bible, YHWH is translated as Kyrios (Greek for "Lord"). In the NT, the word "Kyrios" is used to describe both a normal person (e.g. Eph 6:9.) and Jesus (e.g. 1Cor 6:14).

10.7 Jesus as a mediator between God and the people

The angels, who are mentioned several times over in the Bible, embody the earliest "mediators" in Judaism between God and the people. The Hebrew word for angel is "Malach", which means "messenger".

Chapter 7 has already dealt with the idea that a mediator was necessary between the highest being and the people. Reference was also made to Philo who attributed this task to the logos: "And I (logos) stood in the midst, between the Lord and You; neither being uncreate as God, nor yet created as you, but being in the midst between these two extremities" (her, 42, § 206).

When the logos was transferred to Jesus, he was also assigned the role of a "mediator": "For there is one God; there is also one mediator between God and humankind, Christ Jesus, himself human, who gave himself a ransom for all – this was attested at the right time" (1Ti 2:5-6 NRS).

10.8 Jesus, the Son of Man and the Messiah

The word "Messiah" in the sense of a coming Redeemer does not feature in the Hebrew Bible.

The following prophecies about the advent of the Messiah are included in 1 Enoch:

"In his presence shall they fall, and not be raised up again; nor shall there be any one to take them out of his hands, and to lift them up: for they have denied the Lord of spirits, and his Messiah. The name of the Lord of spirits shall be blessed" (47:11).

"He said, All these things which you behold shall be for the dominion of the **Messiah**, that he may command, and be powerful upon earth" (51:4).

"Then shall the kings, the princes, and all who possess the earth, glorify him who has dominion over all things, him who was concealed; for from the beginning the **Son of man** existed in secret, whom the Most High preserved in the presence of his power, and revealed to the elect" (61:10).

"They shall fix their hopes on this **Son of man**, shall pray to him, and petition him for mercy" (61:14).

As we can see from the above quotations from the First Book of Enoch, "Son of Man" was a messianic title in the 1st century AD as well. As such, the "Son of Man" was deemed to have pre-existed, like the Messiah.

These titles, "Son of Man" and "Messiah" often appear in reference to Jesus in the Gospels but, remarkably enough, not in Paul's Letters. This shows that quite a lot of time still had to pass before the teachings about Jesus were standardized. As will be explained later, the views of the Apostles and their teachings about Christ differed in the various regions of the Roman Empire. In many cases, the titles of "Son of Man" and "Messiah" were not conferred upon Jesus until he was expected to return.

The following prophecy by Zechariah in the Messiah texts of the Qumran scrolls is significant:

"And a second time I said to him "What are these two branches of the olive trees, which pour out the oil through the two golden pipes?" He said to me, "Do you not know what these are?" I said, "No, my lord." Then he said, "These are the two anointed ones who stand by the Lord of the whole earth" (Zec 4:12-14 NRS).

Some parts of the Qumran scrolls, which were probably influenced by the above prophecy, attribute a messianic function to two people – the High Priest and the Leader of this sect, who is named "Teacher of Righteousness" in the CD, 1QpHab and 1Q14 scrolls.

The "anointed one" (Aaron) could also be understood as a Messiah from this textual reference. (4QPB Patriarchal Blessings). 4QS 9,11 also mentions a Messiah of Levi and of Israel.

A "pastoral calendar" dated 9 BC from Priene in Asia Minor shows just how high the expectation of the advent of a superhuman savior was in the second half of the 1st century BC, and not just among the Jews but also in Greek-Roman regions:

"...deeply interested in our life, has set in most perfect order by giving us Augustus, whom she filled with virtue that he might benefit humankind, sending him as a savior both for us and for our descendants, that he might end war and arrange all things, and since he, Caesar, by his appearance excelled even our anticipations, surpassing all previous benefactors, and not even leaving to posterity any hope of surpassing what he has done, and since the birthday of the god Augustus was the beginning of the good tidings for the world that came by reason of him."

The following quotations clearly set the Son of Man on a par with the Messiah: "Now when Jesus came into the district of Caesarea Philippi, he asked his disciples, "Who do people say that the Son of Man is?" And they said, "Some say John the Baptist, but others Elijah, and still others Jeremiah or one of the prophets." He said to them, "But who do you say that I am?" Simon Peter answered "You are the Messiah, the Son of the living God." And Jesus answered him, "Blessed are you, Simon son of Jonah! For flesh and blood has not revealed this to you, but my Father in heaven" (Mat 16:13-17 NRS).

"Again the high priest asked him, "Are you the Messiah, the Son of the Blessed One?" Jesus said "I am; and you will see the Son of Man seated at the right hand of the Power, and coming with the clouds of heaven" (Mar 14:61-62 NRS). (Similarly: Mat 26:63; Joh 10:24.)

The following sentences reflect the opinion that Jesus will only perform the deeds expected in Judaism of a Messiah once he returns and that his return is imminent:

"For the Son of Man is to come with his angels in the glory of his Father, and then he will repay everyone for what has been done. Truly I tell you, there are some standing here who will not taste death before they see the Son of Man coming in his kingdom" (Mat 16:27-28 NRS).

44

The following quotation already offers an explanation for the delay of the Parousia: "...so that times of refreshing may come from the presence of the Lord, and that he may send the Messiah appointed for you, that is, Jesus, who must remain in heaven until the time of universal restoration that God announced long ago through his holy prophets" (Act 3:20-21 NRS).

Justin the Martyr († around 165 AD) sees the return of Jesus already prophesied in the ritual of the Day of Penance:

"And the two goats which were ordered to be offered during the fast, (Lev 16:7-10) of which one was sent away as the scape [goat], and the other sacrificed, were similarly declarative of the two appearances of Christ: the first, in which the elders of your people, and the priests, having laid hands on Him and put Him to death, sent Him away as the scape [goat]; and His second appearance, because in the same place in Jerusalem you shall recognize Him whom you have dishonored, and who was an offering for all sinners willing to repent, and keeping the fast which Isaiah speaks of, loosening the terms of the violent contracts, and keeping the other precepts, likewise enumerated by him, and which I have quoted, which those believing in Jesus do. And further, you are aware that the offering of the two goats, which were enjoined to be sacrificed at the fast, was not permitted to take place similarly anywhere else, but only in Jerusalem" (Dialogue with Trypho 40.4).

The following passage from the Gospel according to Matthew illustrates the good deeds that the Messiah is expected to perform for mankind:

"When John heard in prison what the Messiah was doing, he sent word by his disciples and said to him, "Are you the one who is to come, or are we to wait for another? Jesus answered them, "Go and tell John what you hear and see: the blind receive their sight, the lame walk, the lepers are cleansed, the deaf hear, the dead are raised, and the poor have good news brought to them" (Mat 11:2-5 NRS).

This saying, which is attributed to Jesus, comes from two passages about the messianic expectations in the Hebrew Bible:

"Then the eyes of the blind shall be opened, and the ears of the deaf unstopped, then the lame shall leap like a deer, and the tongue of the speechless sing for joy. For waters shall break forth in the wilderness, and streams in the desert" (Isa 35:5-6 NRS).

And:

"he (the LORD) has sent me to bring good news to the oppressed, to bind up the brokenhearted, to proclaim liberty to the captives, and release to the prisoners" (Isa 61:1 NRS).

The title "Son of God" also indicates that Jesus was accepted into heaven following his passion. As already mentioned earlier on, this title originates from the words of God about the King of Israel:

"…the gospel concerning his Son, who was descended from David according to the flesh and was declared to be Son of God with power according to the spirit of holiness **by** resurrection from the dead, Jesus Christ our Lord" (Rom 1:3-4 NRS). "He will be great, and will be called the Son of the Most High, and the Lord God will give to him the throne of his ancestor David. He will reign over the house of Jacob forever, and of his kingdom there will be no end" (Luk 1:32-33 NRS).

The words passed down as originating from Jesus by Luke the Evangelist are linked to the passion that directly followed: "But from now on the Son of Man will be seated at the right hand of the power of God." All of them asked, "Are you, then, the Son of God?" He said to them, "You say that I am" (Luk 22:69-70 NRS).

John the Evangelist summarized the passion of Jesus in his explanation as follows: "But these are written so that you may come to believe that Jesus is the Messiah, the Son of God, and that through believing you may have life in his name" (Joh 20:31 NRS).

Some passages from the Hebrew Bible that mention the expression "Son of God" were quoted in chapter 7,4. The term "Son of God" was not alien to Jewish philosophy either in the first century CE. The Jewish philosopher Philo, for example, discussed the Son of God as follows: "Having now discussed at sufficient length the subject of change and alteration of names, we will turn to the matters which come next in order in our proposed examination. Immediately after the events which we have just mentioned, came the birth of Isaac; for after God had given to his mother the name of Sarrah instead of Sarah, he said to Abraham, "I will give unto thee a Son" (Gen 17:16.) "We must consider each of the things here indicated particularly. Now he who is properly said to give any thing whatever must by all means be giving what is his own private property. And if this is true beyond controversy, then it would follow that Isaac must not have been a man, but a being synonymous with that most exquisite joy of all pleasures, namely, laughter[14], the adopted **son of God**" (mut.XXIII 130-131, contextual translation).

10.9 Jesus, the Lamb of God

This designation of Jesus is due to John the Baptist. The Gospel according to John mentions twice how John the Baptist called Jesus the "Lamb of God": "The next day he saw Jesus coming toward him and declared, "Here is the Lamb of God who takes away the sin of the world! This is he of whom I said, "After me comes a man who ranks ahead of me because he was before me" (Joh 1:29-30 NRS) (See also 1:36).

These statements contain two references: The first to the Passion ("takes away the sins"), and the second to the pre-existence of Jesus ("because he was before me"). This second statement points to the prediction by the prophet Malachi: "Lo, I will send you the prophet Elijah before the great and terrible day of the LORD comes. He will turn the hearts of parents to their children and the hearts of children to their parents, so that I will not come and strike the land with a curse" (Mal 4:5-6 NRS).

According to Luke 1:17, the archangel Gabriel prophesied to John the Baptist as follows: "With the spirit and power of Elijah he will go before him, to turn the hearts of parents to their children, and the disobedient to the wisdom of the righteous, to make ready a people prepared for the Lord" (Luk 1:17 NRS). This prophecy would have meant that the "day of the LORD" with all its apocalyptic predictions would have happened upon the advent of Jesus.

The fact that this did not come to pass is probably why the identity of John the Baptist as Elijah is questioned in the Gospel according to John: "And they asked him "What then? Are you Elijah?" He said, "I am not" (Joh 1:21 NRS). Chapter 6 of the Revelation sets the Lamb on a par with Jesus.

The use of the term Lamb when describing Jesus is probably connected to the Pessah lamb. The Israelites were only allowed to leave Egypt because God forced the Pharaoh's consent by sending ten plagues. The last of these plagues was the death of each first-born child. God commanded that a lamb be slaughtered to prevent the killing of the first-born children of the Israelites. It is written: "They shall take some of the blood and put it on the two doorposts and the lintel of the houses in which they eat it" (Exo 12:7 NRS).

The association Passion – Pessah – Pessah lamb is very probable, especially when we bear in mind the reference in Revelation: "Then I saw between the throne and the four living creatures and among the elders a Lamb standing as if it had been slaughtered" (Rev 5:6 NRS). By the same token, the lamb is a symbol of innocence, which is sufficient justification for the title being bestowed on Jesus. Especially considering the text by the prophet Isaiah: "He was oppressed, and he was afflicted, yet he did not open his mouth; like a lamb that is led to the slaughter, and like a sheep that before its shearers is silent, so he did not open his mouth" (Isa 53:7 NRS).

See Fig. 1. Mosaic, the Lamb in Paradise with the four paradise rivers, in the apse of St. Zeno's Chapel in Sta Prassede in Rome (early 9th century).

The deer to the left and right symbolize the following verse from the Psalms: "As a deer longs for flowing streams, so my soul longs for you, O God. My soul thirsts for God, for the living God. When shall I come and behold the face of God?" (Psa 42:1-2 NRS).

10.10 Jesus, the second or last Adam

Paul emphasizes the parallels between Jesus and Adam several times. By comparing the two he draws conclusions about the special nature of Jesus that is bestowed on everyone who makes it to heaven:

"for as all die in Adam, so all will be made alive in Christ. But each in his own order: Christ the first fruits, then at his coming those who belong to Christ" Then comes the end, when he hands over the kingdom to God the Father, after he has destroyed every ruler and every authority and power. For he must reign until he has put all his enemies under his feet. The last enemy to be destroyed is death. (1Co 15:22-26 NRS).

Paul continues: "Thus it is written, "The first man, Adam, became a living being"; the last Adam became a life-giving spirit. But it is not the spiritual that is first, but the physical, and then the spiritual. The first man was from the earth, a man of dust; the second man is from heaven. As was the man of dust, so are those who are of the dust; and as is the man of heaven, so are those who are of heaven. Just as we have borne the image of the man of dust, we will also bear the image of the man of heaven" (1Co 15:45-49 NRS).

Equally, Paul writes to the Romans, 5,12 et seqq: "Therefore, just as sin came into the world through one man, and death came through sin, and so death spread to all because all have sinned – sin was indeed in the world before the law, but sin is not reckoned when there is no law. Yet death exercised dominion from Adam to Moses, even over those whose sins were not like the transgression of

Adam, who is a type of the one who was to come. But the free gift is not like the trespass. For if the many died through the one man's trespass, much more surely have the grace of God and the free gift in the grace of the one man, Jesus Christ, abounded for the many" (Rom 5:12-15 NRS).

Augustine of Hippo (354 - 430 AD) was prompted by these words of Paul to develop his teachings of original sin. Mankind can opt for the path of good, despite original sin, but only with the help of God's mercy. Mankind is redeemed through the sacrament of baptism since the baptized are freed from original sin. In mortal life, however, it still has to deal with the consequences of original sin.

The Greek term "ἐφ᾽ ᾧ (Rom 5:12 BNT)" (translated as "because" in the standardized translation; literally: "for this reason, it") from Rom. 5:12 was quoted in the Vulgate, the Latin translation of the Bible, as "in quo", meaning in him (Adam) has all mankind sinned. It was this translation that led Augustine of Hippo, who can be deemed the father of the teachings of original sin, to his belief that sin is hereditary.[15]

Origen (185 - 254 AD) reports on a tradition he learned from Judaism that Adam was buried on Calvary (Golgotha). He reinforces the comparison between Adam and Jesus by opining that Christ's cross was erected on a spot directly above Adam's grave.[16]

The legend quoted by Origen has not been found in Jewish tradition to this day. Chapters 16 and 23 of the apocryphal scripture "The Cave of Treasures" (original title: Syriac "Me'arath Gazze)[17], which was possibly based on a Jewish original, recount that Methusalem, one of the patriarchs and the oldest person to have ever lived on earth, gave instructions to Noah and his descendants. In keeping with these instructions, Sem and Melchizedek buried Adam's corpse in the centre of the earth many centuries later. In the 4th and 5th centuries – the time during which the scripture was probably written – the centre of earth was deemed to be Calvary. The legend recounts: "And Shem took the body of Adam and Melchisedek, and went forth by night from among his people, and behold, the Angel of the Lord, who was going before them, appeared unto them. And their journey was very speedy, because the Angel of the Lord strengthened them until they arrived at that place. And when they arrived at Gâghûltâ (Golgotha), which is the centre of the earth, the Angel of the Lord showed Shem the place [for the body of Adam]. And when Shem had deposited the body of our father Adam upon that place [Fol. 21a, col. 2], the four quarters [of the earth] separated themselves from each other, and the earth opened itself in the form of a cross, and Shem and Melchizedek deposited the body of Adam there (i.e. in the cavity). And as soon as they had laid it therein, the four quarters [of the earth] drew quickly together, and enclosed the body of our father Adam, and the door of the created world was shut fast. And that place was called "Karkaphtâ " (i.e.

"Skull"), because the head of all the children of men was deposited there. And it was called "Gâghûltâ," because it was round [like the head], and "Resîphtâ" (i.e. a trodden-down thing), because the head of the accursed serpent, that is to say, Satan, was crushed there, and "Gefîftâ " (Gabbatha), because all the nations were to be gathered together to it".[18]

The Church of the Holy Sepulcher at the foot of Calvary in Jerusalem houses the Greek Orthodox Adam's Chapel. This is where Adam's skull apparently lay. According to one legend, the blood of Jesus dripped through a crack in the rocks on to the skull, thus freeing Adam from original sin. This story is apparently proven by a rock next to Adam's Chapel, which is colored red in places.[19]

See Fig. 2. Fra Angelico, section from the Crucifixion, fresco in San Marco in Florence: around 1437–1446, Florence, Museo di San Marco.

The author was unfortunately unable to identify the source of this legend; it does not feature in the "Legenda aurea" by Jacobus de Voragine (around 1230 –1298 AD).

The terms first and second Adam were also known in Judaism. The Kabbalist Isaac Luria (1534 – 1572 AD) conceived that this first Adam was Adam Kadmon. He was styled as the primal man on whom earthly humans were imaged. Earthly humans, however, lost the three wisdoms that placed Adam Kadmon alongside God – wisdom, reverence and immortality. It should be noted that Kabbalah is one of the doctrines in Judaism. It is practiced by only a few and is rejected by many Jews.

10.11 Jesus, the logos

Philo's interpretation, which assumed that logos was a "second God", has already been addressed in chapter 8.

Paul also hinted at a possible pre-existence of Jesus: "yet for us there is one God, the Father, from whom are all things and for whom we exist, and one Lord, Jesus Christ, through whom are all things and through whom we exist" (1Co 8:6 NRS). Additionally: "Thus it is written "The first man, Adam, became a living being" (Gen 2,7); the last Adam became a life-giving spirit. "But it is not the spiritual that is first, but the physical, and then the spiritual. The first man was from the (Adam – adamah hebr. earth) earth, a man of dust; the second man is from heaven" (1Co 15:45-47NRS).

Paul might possibly have been familiar with Philo's work and therefore influenced by the idea of a pre-existent logos. The Gospels according to Mark, Matthew and Luke do not contain any references to this fundamental idea. This shows how locally contained the understanding of the teachings of Jesus were, and how they differed over time.

Since the logos was equated to Jesus in the Prologue of the Gospel according to John, the adoption of the pre-existence of Jesus into Christian doctrine was a logical consequence. This statement is clearly found in a later Deutero-Pauline Letter: "He (Jesus) is the image of the invisible God, the firstborn of all creation; for in him all things in heaven and on earth were created, things visible and invisible, whether thrones or dominions or rulers or powers – all things have been created through him and for him. He himself is before all things, and in him all things hold together" (Col 1:15-17 NRS).

In keeping with the description of Jesus as logos in 1:1-15 in the Gospel according to John, his pre-existence is emphasized in several places: "Jesus said to them, "Very truly, I tell you, before Abraham was, I am" (Joh 8:58 NRS). "So now, Father, glorify me in your own presence with the glory that I had in your presence before the world existed" (Joh 17:5 NRS). "Father, I desire that those also, whom you have given me, may be with me where I am, to see my glory, which you have given me because you loved me before the foundation of the world" (Joh 17:24 NRS).

Justin continues to develop this view, as can be seen in the Dialogue with Trypho, 62,2 et seqq: "He (God) said: "Let Us make man after our image and likeness" (Gen 1:26). Justin raises the question as to whether God was talking to Himself and finds proof of the logos, to which this demand was addressed, in the following: "And that you may not change the [force of the] words just quoted, and repeat what your teachers assert – either that God said to Himself, "Let Us make", just as we, when about to do something, oftentimes say to ourselves, 'Let us make;' or that God spoke to the elements, to wit, the earth and other similar substances of which we believe man was formed, "Let Us make", – I shall quote again the words narrated by Moses himself, from which we can indisputably learn that [God] conversed with some one who was numerically distinct from Himself, and also a rational Being. These are the words: "And God said, "Behold, Adam has become as one of us, to know good and evil" (Gen 3:22). In saying, therefore, 'as one of us,' [Moses] has declared that [there is a certain] number of persons associated with one another, and that they are at least two. For I would not say that the dogma of that heresy which is said to be among you is true, or that the teachers of it can prove that [God] spoke to angels, or that the human frame was the workmanship of angels. But this Offspring, which was truly brought forth from the Father, was with the Father before all the creatures, and the Father communed with Him; even as the Scripture by Solomon has made clear, that He whom Solomon calls Wisdom, was begotten as a Beginning before all His creatures and as Offspring by God,... and they call Him the Word (logos), because He carries tidings from the Father to men: but maintain that this power is indivisible and inseparable from the Father, just as they say that the light of the sun on earth is indivisible and inseparable from the sun in the heavens; as when it sinks, the light sinks along with it" (Justin, Dialogue with Trypho the Jew, 128).

Justin refers in his quotation to the "Scripture by Solomon", meaning the Book of Wisdom, which was traditionally attributed to Solomon. There, it says: "I will tell you what wisdom is and how she came to be, and I will hide no secrets from you, but I will trace her course from the beginning of creation, and make knowledge of her clear, and I will not pass by the truth" (Wis 6:22 NRS).

"I shall give you another testimony, my friends, from the Scriptures, that God begot before all creatures a Beginning, [who was] a certain rational power [proceeding] from Himself, who is called by the Holy Spirit, now the Glory of the Lord, now the Son, again Wisdom, again an Angel, then God, and then Lord and Logos; and on another occasion He calls Himself Captain, when He appeared in human form to Joshua the son of Nave (Nun). For He can be called by all those names, since He ministers to the Father's will, and since He was begotten of the Father by an act of will" (Justin - Dialogue with Trypho the Jew, 61,1-6).

Justin's reference to the Captain who appeared to Joshua is recorded in the Book of Joshua: "Once when Joshua was by Jericho, he looked up and saw a man standing before him with a drawn sword in his hand. Joshua went to him and said to him, "Are you one of us, or one of our adversaries?" He replied, "Neither; but as commander of the army of the LORD I have now come." And Joshua fell on his face to the earth and worshipped, and he said to him "What do you command your servant, my lord?" (Jos 5:13-14 NRS).

Clement of Alexandria, around 150 - around 215 AD clearly identified the logos as Jesus in "the Protrepticus" ("Exhortation to the Greeks") I.6.1.

10.12 Jesus, the God

The following sentences are understood by Jews to be homage to the King, whereas Christians interpret them as a prediction that Jesus is the Son of God. The Kings' Psalms, above all, were used as references for such predictions about Jesus: "I will tell of the decree of the LORD: He said to me, "You are my son; today I have begotten you" (Psa 2:7 NRS).

And:

"The LORD says to my lord, "Sit at my right hand until I make your enemies your footstool" (Psa 110:1 NRS).[20]

Similar intimations were, however, discovered in other Books of the Hebrew Bible. e.g.: "...I (God) will establish the throne of his (Solomon's) kingdom forever. I will be a father to him, and he shall be a son to me. When he commits iniquity, I will punish him with a rod such as mortals use, with blows inflicted by human beings. But I will not take my steadfast love from him" (2Sa 7b:13-15a NRS).

Paul also seems to have considered that Jesus may have been God as can be concluded from a remark in his Letter to the Phillippians, 2,6: "though he (Jesus) was in the form of God, did not regard equality with God as something to be exploited, but emptied himself, taking the form of a slave, being born in human likeness. And being found in human form, he humbled himself and became obedient to the point of death – even death on a cross. Therefore God also highly exalted him and gave him the name that is above every name, so that at the name of Jesus every knee should bend, in heaven and on earth and under the earth, and every tongue should confess that Jesus Christ is Lord, to the glory of God the Father" (Phi 2:6-11 NRS).

The aforementioned sentence implies that proskynesis formed part of the ritual of revering Jesus. Jews who did not believe in Jesus were unable to grasp this concept of bended knee.

A subordination of Jesus was derived from the following sentence by Paul, for example: "yet for us there is one God, the Father, from whom are all things and for whom we exist, and one Lord, Jesus Christ, through whom are all things and through whom we exist" (1Co 8:6 NRS). This opinion was clarified in the Nicene Creed (325 AD): It begins: "I believe in one God, the Father almighty, maker of heaven and earth, and of all things visible and invisible. And in one Lord, Jesus Christ, the only begotten Son of God, born of the Father before all ages. God from God, Light from Light, true God from true God, begotten, not made, one in being with the Father; through Whom all things were made"

Paul saw no justification for claiming that his teachings about the nature of Jesus represented a departure from the Jewish monotheistic faith. He emphasizes: "...since God is one; and he will justify the circumcised on the ground of faith and the uncircumcised through that same faith. Do we then overthrow the law by this faith? By no means! On the contrary, we uphold the law" (Rom 3:30-31 NRS). And:

"For from him (God) and through him and to him are all things. To him be the glory forever" (Rom 11:36 NRS).

Paul believed that the Son's rule would only last until the end of the world. He emphasizes his monotheist view by believing that only God will come as the sole, superhuman ruler when the world ends:

"Then comes the end, when he hands over the kingdom to God the Father, after he has destroyed every ruler and every authority and power. For he must reign until he has put all his enemies under his feet. The last enemy to be destroyed is death. For God has put all things in subjection under his feet. But when it says, All things are put in subjection, it is plain that this does not include the one who put all things in subjection under him. When all things are subjected to him, then the Son himself will also be subjected to the one who put all things in subjection under him, so that God may be all in all" (1Co 15:24-28 NRS).

The following sentence from the Gospel according to Matthew implies a subordination of Jesus vis-à-vis the "Holy Spirit", which was amended, at the latest, in the Nicene Creed as already quoted above.

"Whoever speaks a word against the Son of Man will be forgiven, but whoever speaks against the Holy Spirit will not be forgiven, either in this age or in the age to come" (Mat 12:32 NRS).

The Gospel according to Matthew also holds the view of a certain closeness of Jesus to God, as illustrated by the following quotation:

"The Son of Man will send his angels, and they will collect out of his kingdom all causes of sin and all evildoers, and they will throw them into the furnace of fire, where there will be weeping and gnashing of teeth. Then the righteous will shine like the sun in the kingdom of their Father. Let anyone with ears listen!" (Mat 13:41-43 NRS). Similarly: "For the Son of Man is to come with his angels in the glory of his Father, and then he will repay everyone for what has been done" (Mat 16:27 NRS).

The Gospel according to John virtually places Jesus on a par with God: "Indeed, just as the Father raises the dead and gives them life, so also the Son gives life to whomever he wishes. The Father judges no one but has given all judgment to the Son, so that all may honor the Son just as they honor the Father. Anyone who does not honor the Son does not honor the Father who sent him" (Joh 5:21-23 NRS).

Equally: "Thomas answered him, "My Lord and my God!" (Joh 20:28 NRS). God can be seen as an honorary title (cf. chapter 7.3) although this saying was later interpreted as the outcome of divine inspiration.

If John the Evangelist had already recognized Jesus as the true God, then he probably would have expressed this belief in other places in his Gospel, and the statement made in the First Letter of Clement (quoted further down) would have been unfounded.

In the Letter to the Hebrews, which was probably written between 60 and 90 AD, the name "Jesus" (Hebrew: "Jehoschua" (God is Redemption)) is used to prove his high heavenly ranking:

"Long ago God spoke to our ancestors in many and various ways by the prophets, but in these last days he has spoken to us by a Son, whom he appointed heir of all things, through whom he also created the worlds. He is the reflection of God's glory and the exact imprint of God's very being, and he sustains all things by his powerful word. When he had made purification for sins, he sat down at the right hand of the Majesty on high, having become as much superior to angels as the name he has inherited is more excellent than theirs. For to which of the angels did God ever say, "You are my Son; today I have begotten you?" Or again, "I will be his Father, and he will be my Son?" And again, when he brings the firstborn into the world, he says, "Let all God's angels worship him." Of the angels he says "He makes his angels winds, and his servants flames of fire." But of the Son he says, "Your throne, O God, is forever and ever, and the righteous scepter is the scepter of your kingdom" (Heb 1:1-8 NRS). These sentences show that the divine nature of Christ was possibly a consideration in the 1st century AD but had not yet become an integral part of Christology.

It was not until Second Clement in 150 AD that the possible worship of Jesus as God was considered:

"1. Brethren, we ought so to think of Jesus Christ, as of God, as of the Judge of quick and dead."

11. Why was Jesus crucified?

The following quotation shows that Jews under Roman rule were not allowed to pass death sentences: "Pilate said to them, "Take him yourselves and judge him according to your law." The Jews replied, "We are not permitted to put anyone to death" (Joh 18:31 NRS).

The Romans only crucified criminals found guilty of capital offences. Insurgency against the Emperor was deemed to be such a capital offence, which is what Jesus committed by claiming the title of King for himself. As Josephus Flavius (37 or 38 – c. 100 AD) mentions, high-ranking Jews usually intervened to try and help their fellow believers who had been brought before a Roman tribunal. The Gospels show why the opposite was more the case with Jesus:

"So the chief priests and the Pharisees called a meeting of the council, and said, "What are we to do? This man is performing many signs. If we let him go on like this, everyone will believe in him, and the Romans will come and destroy both our holy place and our nation." But one of them, Caiaphas, who was high priest that year, said to them, "You know nothing at all! You do not understand that it is better for you to have one man die for the people than to have the whole nation destroyed" (Joh 11:47-50 NRS).

One might now rightfully ask why it possible to blame Jesus for the destruction of a "whole nation". The following answer can be found in the Acts: "For some time ago Theudas (Josephus Flavius, Antiquities of the Jews 20,5,1) rose up, claiming to be somebody, and a number of men, about four hundred, joined him; but he was killed, and all who followed him were dispersed and disappeared. After him Judas the Galilean rose up at the time of the census and got people to follow him; he also perished, and all who followed him were scattered" (Act 5:36-37 NRS).

In his work "The Wars of the Jews" II, 17,8 et seq, Josephus Flavius also mentions Menachem, son of Judas from Galilea, who claimed to be a Messiah and who was also defeated in battle by the Romans, along with his comrades.

The High Council seems to have feared that Jesus' claim of being the Messiah could equally culminate in revolt against the Romans, which is why they did not intervene with Pilate to help him. It was probably the messianic claim by Jesus, which was linked to the title of King, that prompted Pilate to pass the sentence of death that was commensurate with a capital offence.

The Evangelists wanted to shift the burden of guilt from the Romans to the Jews. This assumption is probably true because the Christians may have wanted to establish as much comity with the ruling Romans as possible.

Pilate's gesture of letting the people decide whether Barabbas or Jesus should be executed in order to save Jesus, which is narrated in all four Gospels, is highly improbable. "Now at the festival the governor was accustomed to release a prisoner for the crowd, anyone whom they wanted" (Mat 27:15 NRS), (equally: Mar 15:6; Luk 23:18; Joh 18:39).

According to the Evangelists' accounts, this was not a one-off gesture, but one that was repeated every year. If this were historically credible, there would be some reference to this procedure in either Jewish or Roman accounts. Despite the efforts of many researchers, not even the slightest hint that would prove this tradition has been found.

In the absence of a charismatic "Messiah", the crucifixion of the "Messiah" also removed the threat of one of Jesus' disciples inciting an uprising, which is why the Apostles were not persecuted after Jesus' execution.

12. Christian arguments for justifying the crucifixion of Jesus

The crucifixion posed a development that the disciples of Jesus, who worshipped him as the Messiah, were unable to explain. The promise of his resurrection and ascension to heaven and the covenant that he would return were, however, powerful proof to the believers that Jesus was the anticipated Messiah. Especially since the Hebrew Bible contained prophecies by Isaiah that could be interpreted as references to Jesus' fate. These were the Songs of the Suffering Servant (Isaiah 52:13-53:12), which the Jews believed symbolized the fate of the nation of Israel: "He was despised and rejected by others; a man of suffering and acquainted with infirmity; and as one from whom others hide their faces he was despised, and we held him of no account. Surely he has borne our infirmities and carried our diseases; yet we accounted him stricken, struck down by God, and afflicted. (See chapter 19 for the interpretation of the word " חָלַל ".) But he was wounded for our transgressions, crushed for our iniquities; upon him was the punishment that made us whole, and by his bruises we are healed. All we like sheep have gone astray; we have all turned to our own way, and the LORD has laid on him the iniquity of us all. He was oppressed, and he was afflicted, yet he did not open his mouth; like a lamb that is led to the slaughter, and like a sheep that before its shearers is silent, so he did not open his mouth. By a perversion of justice he was taken away. Who could have imagined his future? For he was cut off from the land of the living, stricken for the transgression of my people. They made his grave with the wicked and his tomb with the rich, although he had done no violence, and there was no deceit in his mouth. Yet it was the will of the LORD to crush him with pain. When you make his life an offering for sin, he shall see his offspring, and shall prolong his days; through him the will of the LORD shall prosper" (Isa 53:3-10 NRS).

In a later phase, whose origins cannot be traced, the scribes attributed the quoted passage to the Messiah ben Ephraim or ben Joseph. This Messiah was apparently to suffer death and prepare the way for the Messiah ben David who would bring final redemption. This belief of a second Messiah was possibly influenced by the Passion of Jesus, although this is primarily considered to have been the death of Bar Kochba, who was also seen as a Messiah and who led the revolution in 132 -135 AD.

13. The resurrection of Jesus

"When he had said this, as they were watching, he was lifted up, and a cloud took him out of their sight. While he was going and they were gazing up toward heaven, suddenly two men in white robes stood by them. They said, "Men of Galilee, why do you stand looking up toward heaven? This Jesus, who has been taken up from you into heaven, will come in the same way as you saw him go into heaven" (Act 1:9-11 NRS).

"While he was blessing them, he withdrew from them and was carried up into heaven" (Luk 24:51 NRS).

Jesus' ascension into heaven as narrated in Acts 1:9 et seqq and in Luke cannot be compared with other "ascensions", such as Elijah in the whirlwind (2 Kings 2:11) or the rapture of Paul since Jesus had died and risen again. Paul himself describes the rapture and his return: "I know a person in Christ who fourteen years ago was caught up to the third heaven – whether in the body or out of the body I do not know; God knows. And I know that such a person – whether in the body or out of the body I do not know; God knows – was caught up into Paradise and heard things that are not to be told, that no mortal is permitted to repeat" (2Co 12:2-4 NRS).

Justin the Martyr draws on Greek mythology for parallels to Jesus' acceptance into heaven to make it easier for heathens to understand:

"And when we say also that the Word (logos=Jesus), who is the first-born. of God, was produced without sexual union, and that He, Jesus Christ, our Teacher, was crucified and died, and rose again, and ascended into heaven, we propound nothing different from what you believe regarding those whom you esteem sons of Jupiter. For you know how many sons your esteemed writers ascribed to Jupiter: Mercury, the interpreting word and teacher of all; Æsculapius, who, though he was a great physician, was struck by a thunderbolt, and so ascended to heaven; and Bacchus too, after he had been torn limb from limb; and Hercules, when he had committed himself to the flames to escape his toils; and the sons of Leda, and Dioscuri; and Perseus, son of Danae; and Bellerophon, who, though sprung from mortals, rose to heaven on the horse Pegasus. For what shall I say of Ariadne, and those who, like her, have been declared to be set among the stars? And what of the emperors who die among yourselves, whom you deem worthy of deification, and in whose behalf you produce some one who swears he has seen the burning Cæsar rise to heaven from the funeral pyre? And what kind of deeds are recorded of each of these reputed sons of Jupiter, it is needless to tell to those who already know. This only shall be said, that they are written for the advantage and encouragement. ...But far be such a thought concerning the gods from every well-conditioned soul, as to believe that Jupiter himself, the governor and creator of all things, was both a parricide and the son of a parricide, and that being overcome by the love of base and shameful pleasures, he came in to Ganymede and those many women whom he had violated and that his sons did like actions. But, as we said above, wicked devils perpetrated these things. And we have learned that those only are deified who have lived near to God in holiness and virtue; and we believe that those who live wickedly and do not repent are punished in everlasting fire" (The First Apology, 21).

14. The explanation for the resurrection of Jesus

"King Herod heard of it, for Jesus' name had become known. Some were saying "John the baptizer has been raised from the dead; and for this reason these powers are at work in him." But others said "It is Elijah." And others said "It is a prophet, like one of the prophets of old." But when Herod heard of it, he said "John, whom I beheaded, has been raised" (Mar 6:14-16 NRS).

The opinion that Moses had also ascended was widely held in the 1st century AD ("The Ascension of Moses"). Similar accounts may have been told of other prophets who ascended. They have not, however, survived.

The aforementioned quotations show that it was not unusual to believe in ascension in the 1st century AD.

The Second Coming of Christ (also Second Advent or Parousia) that is promised in the Gospel according to John is linked to the Holy Spirit who was charged with watching over the Christians until Jesus' return. This is why statements referring to the Holy Spirit are particularly significant. "But the Advocate, the Holy Spirit, whom the Father will send in my name, will teach you everything, and remind you of all that I have said to you" (Joh 14:26 NRS). "I (Jesus) will not leave you orphaned; I am coming to you. In a little while the world will no longer see me, but you will see me; because I live, you also will live. On that day you will know that I am in my Father, and you in me, and I in you" (Joh 14:18-20 NRS). This verse implies that Jesus' disciples will be blessed upon his return.

15. The resurrection of the dead

The resurrection of the dead forms an integral part of the faith, not only of Christianity but also of Judaism.

Judaism originally believed in the unity of a person, i.e. that the soul was not separate from the body. For example: "then the LORD God formed man from the dust of the ground, and breathed into his nostrils the breath of life; and the man became a living being" (Gen 2:7 NRS). Certain passages in the Hebrew Bible quote the word "soul" independently of the word "heart" which usually meant the body. The "soul" in this case refers to people's emotions or to people as a whole.[21]

Stoicism, which – as already mentioned – influenced Judaism from the 3rd century BC onwards, only made a relative distinction between matter and soul. They claimed that the soul was just fine-particled matter with a fiery substance.[22] This approximates to the Jewish belief that the soul was a material substance.

A resurrection of the body with soul can be gleaned from the following passages in the Hebrew Bible: "Come, let us return to the LORD; for it is he who has torn, and he will heal us; he has struck down, and he will bind us up. After two days he will revive us; on the third day he will raise us up, that we may live before him" (Hos 6:1-2 NRS).

According to this prophecy, Jesus predicted that he would rise again three days after he had died: "…the Pharisees gathered before Pilate and said "Sir, we remember what that impostor said while he was still alive, "After three days I will rise again" (Mat 27:62-63 NRS).

Further references to the resurrection of the dead can be found in the following quotations from the Books of Isaiah and Daniel in the Hebrew Bible: "he will swallow up death forever. Then the Lord GOD will wipe away the tears from all faces, and the disgrace of his people he will take away from all the earth, for the LORD has spoken. It will be said on that day ,Lo, this is our God; we have waited for him, so that he might save us. This is the LORD for whom we have waited; let us be glad and rejoice in his salvation" (Isa 25:8-9 NRS).

"Your dead shall live, **their corpses shall rise**. O dwellers in the dust, awake and sing for joy! For your dew is a radiant dew, and the earth will give birth to those long dead" (Isa 26:19 NRS). This quotation explains why the Jews forbid cremation of the dead.

"Many of those who sleep in the dust of the earth shall awake, some to everlasting life, and some to shame and everlasting contempt. Those who are wise shall shine like the brightness of the sky, and those who lead many to righteousness, like the stars forever and ever" (Dan 12:2-3 NRS). This passage implies the existence of heaven and hell. The Hebrew word for hell – Ge-Hinnom – was originally the name of a place in biblical Judah. In the Hellenist era the name was transferred in prophetic writings (Jeremiah 7:30–8:3 and in the pseudepigraphical works 1 Enoch, 4th Book of Esra and in the Sibylline Oracles) to a place of punishment that resembled hell.

In respect of the scriptures 1 Enoch[23], the Book of Jubilees[24], and the Testament of the Twelve Patriarchs[25], Kurt Schubert remarks that "soul" or "spirit" was always fundamentally endowed with bodily characteristics. As such, statements that point to a resurrection of the soul alone actually mean the resurrection of a soul with bodily functions.[26]

According to the following apocryphal scriptures, the soul can temporarily separate from the body: The Apocalypse of Zephaniah, which deals with the fate of the dead (Richard Bauckham assumes that it was written in pre-Christian times[27]), narrates how Zephaniah's soul leaves his body in order to follow the route taken by the souls of the dead. Following the vision, his soul returns to his body, thus enabling him to recount his journey.[28]

Resurrection is not mentioned in the "Apocalypse of Abraham"[29], although it does indicate two types of restoration: An apocalyptic restoration of earth at the end of time, and one of the Garden of Eden as the heavenly paradise where the just go when they die (29:15-18).[30] The 4th Book of the Sibylline Oracles[31] (181-191 AD) the pious are promised bodily resurrection in this world where "they shall see each other".

These aforementioned representations prompted Lohfink to summaries as follows: A life outside the body, as propagated in the anthropology of the Old Testament, is scarcely possible in the Jewish apocalypse.[32]

Philo distinguishes between a legitimate and an illegitimate ascension of the soul. The ascension of souls of the Jewish people, and especially of Moses, was legitimate; the attempt to break into heaven through the construction of the Tower of Babel or the apotheosis of Emperor Gaius Caligula was illegitimate.[33]

Josephus Flavius understood the immortality of the soul as an ethically neutral, inherent characteristic. In his work "The War of the Jews" he writes: "The bodies of all men are indeed mortal, and are created out of corruptible matter; but the soul is ever immortal, and is a portion of the divinity that inhabits our bodies" (III,8,5); "it was a glorious thing to die for the laws of their country; because that the soul was immortal, and that an eternal enjoyment of happiness did await such as died on that account" (I,33,2).

64

He also documented his belief about bodily resurrection in his work "Antiquities of the Jews": "They (the Pharisees[34]) also believe that souls have an immortal rigor in them, and that under the earth there will be rewards or punishments, according as they have lived virtuously or viciously in this life; and the latter are to be detained in an everlasting prison, but that the former shall have power to revive and live again" (XVIII,1,3).

In his speech in Jotpata, when some of his team preferred to commit suicide rather than being taken prisoner by the Romans, Josephus asks the rhetorical question: "and why do we set our soul and body, which are such dear companions, at such variance?" (The War of the Jews III,8,5)[35] Hans Cavallin writes: "Anyway, it's quite clear that the separation of body and soul here, in sharp contrast to the Platonic view is and is understood as a punishment."[36] This also reflected the Rabbinical view.[37] This could also be a reason for the facilitated adoption of the Hellenist ideas about the soul.

In the 1st or 2nd century BC, one of the Qumran scrolls expects bodily resurrection for everyone (4Q521, col 2,12.).

According to the following quotations, which also date from this period, only the just could expect resurrection:

"One cannot but choose to die at the hands of mortals and to cherish the hope God gives of being raised again by him. But for you there will be no resurrection to life!" (2Ma 7:14 NRS).[38] This quotation is taken from a legend, according to which Syrian King Antiochus IV Epiphanes tried to convince seven sons and their mother to disavow Judaism by torturing them so severely that they died. These words were spoken to the King by the fourth son.

Paul confines resurrection to the Christians: "But in fact Christ has been raised from the dead, the first fruits of those who have died. For since death came through a human being, the resurrection of the dead has also come through a human being; for as all die in Adam, so all will be made alive in Christ. But each in his own order: Christ the first fruits, then at his coming those who belong to Christ" (1Co 15:20-23 NRS).

Luke the Evangelist, who is assumed to have written the Acts, teaches the resurrection of everyone: "But this I admit to you, that according to the Way, which they call a sect, I worship the God of our ancestors, believing everything laid down according to the law or written in the prophets. I have a hope in God – a hope that they themselves also accept – that there will be a resurrection of both the righteous and the unrighteous" (Act 24:14-15 NRS).

In explaining their teachings about resurrection, Mark and Luke refer to the resurrection of the dead in the Hebrew Bible:

"And as for the dead being raised, have you not read in the book of Moses, in the story about the bush, how God said to him, "I am the God of Abraham, the

God of Isaac, and the God of Jacob"? He is God not of the dead, but of the living" (Mar 12:26-27 NRS, similarly: Luke 20:37).

The events predicted by the prophets that were expected of Jesus as a Messiah – such as national independence and eternal peace – did not materialize. As these expectations were disappointed, and in order not to raise doubts about the messianity of Jesus, the conclusion was drawn that the messianic work would not be completed until after Jesus' return. The prophet Malachi had already predicted such a return of holy men to Israel: "Lo, I will send you the prophet Elijah before the great and terrible day of the LORD comes" (Mal 4:5 NRS).

The hope of all Christians to continue life near God is linked to the return of Jesus:

"And if I go and prepare a place for you, I will come again and will take you to myself, so that where I am, there you may be also" (Joh 14:3 NRS).

16. Expectations of the imminent return of Jesus

As illustrated by the following quotations from the New Testament, Jesus' disciples expected him to return imminently.

"For this we declare to you by the word of the Lord, that we who are alive, who are left until the coming of the Lord, will by no means precede those who have died. For the Lord himself, with a cry of command, with the archangel's call and with the sound of God's trumpet, will descend from heaven, and the dead in Christ will rise first. Then we who are alive, who are left, will be caught up in the clouds together with them to meet the Lord in the air; and so we will be with the Lord forever. Therefore encourage one another with these words" (1Thess 4:15-18 NRS).

And: "Truly I tell you, there are some standing here who will not taste death before they see the Son of Man coming in his kingdom" (Mat 16:28 NRS). The older saying "Our Lord, come", which was prompted by the certainty of the expected resurrection, was turned into a request to Jesus to come soon.

The use of an Aramaic expression for the return of Jesus by Paul in a letter to the Greek speaking disciples of Jesus in Corinth shows that the following saying was influenced by the Jewish-Christian narrative: "Let anyone be accursed who has no love for the Lord. Our Lord, come!" (1Co 16:22 NRS). In the Greek original and in some translations the Aramaic expression "Marana tha" for "Our Lord, come" is mentioned. This Aramaic inclusion in the original Greek text shows that this expression emerged in the period after Jesus' crucifixion and represented a short prayer in the Christian congregations in Asia Minor and Palestine. Aramaic was the lingua franca in these regions.

In the same context: "The one who testifies to these things says, "Surely I am coming soon." Amen. Come, Lord Jesus!" (Rev 22:20 NRS).

The following sentence shows that doubts arose about the expectation of imminent return: "But if that wicked slave says to himself, "My master is delayed", and he begins to beat his fellow slaves, and eats and drinks with drunkards, the master of that slave will come on a day when he does not expect him and at an hour that he does not know. He will cut him in pieces and put him with the hypocrites, where there will be weeping and gnashing of teeth" (Mat 24:48-51NRS).

17. Delay in the return of Jesus

The following sentence indicates an apocalyptic influence. It voices the belief that a cosmic natural catastrophe must first strike the world before everyone is then resurrected on the Day of Judgment:

"But by the same word the present heavens and earth have been reserved for fire, being kept until the day of judgment and destruction of the godless. But do not ignore this one fact, beloved, that with the Lord one day is like a thousand years, and a thousand years are like one day. The Lord is not slow about his promise, as some think of slowness, but is patient with you, not wanting any to perish, but all to come to repentance. But the day of the Lord will come like a thief, and then the heavens will pass away with a loud noise, and the elements will be dissolved with fire, and the earth and everything that is done on it will be disclosed. Since all these things are to be dissolved in this way, what sort of persons ought you to be in leading lives of holiness and godliness, waiting for and hastening the coming of the day of God" (2Pe 3:7-12).

The following explanation is most commonly used as the reason why Jesus did not return: "So when they had come together, they asked him "Lord, is this the time when you will restore the kingdom to Israel?" He replied, "It is not for you to know the times or periods that the Father has set by his own authority. But you will receive power when the Holy Spirit has come upon you; and you will be my witnesses in Jerusalem, in all Judea and Samaria, and to the ends of the earth" (Act 1:6-8 NRS).

The Catholic Church explicitly links Parusia to the Last Judgment in its Catechism issued in 2003 (Latin, Vatican 1997): "1038: The resurrection of all the dead, "of both the just and the unjust,"[39] will precede the Last Judgment. This will be "the hour when all who are in the tombs will hear [the Son of man's] voice and come forth, those who have done good, to the resurrection of life, and those who have done evil, to the resurrection of judgment."[40] Then Christ will come "in his glory, and all the angels with him. Before him will be gathered all the nations, and he will separate them one from another as a shepherd separates the sheep from the goats, and he will place the sheep at his right hand, but the goats at the left. And they will go away into eternal punishment, but the righteous into eternal life".[41]

18. The redemption

This expression is used with multiple meanings in the Hebrew Bible: For example, in Exo 6:6, redemption means release from Egyptian capture. Psa 25:22 states: "Redeem Israel, O God, out of all its troubles" (Psa 25:22 NRS). Psa 30:3 et seq links redemption to an individual plight: "Incline your ear to me; rescue me speedily. Be a rock of refuge for me, a strong fortress to save me. You are indeed my rock and my fortress; for your name's sake lead me and guide me, take me out of the net that is hidden for me, for you are my refuge. Into your hand I commit my spirit; you have redeemed me, O LORD, faithful God" (Psa 31:2-5 NRS). The term "redemption" is given a new meaning in Psa 130:8b, by expressing the expectation that God "will redeem Israel from all its iniquities".

This redemption from punishment for sins that have been committed is first induced by offering sacrifices in Israel, whereby different sacrifices were made in atonement, depending on the sin committed.

The following is an example: "And you shall bring to the LORD, as your penalty for the sin that you have committed, a female from the flock, a sheep or a goat, as a sin offering; and the priest shall make atonement on your behalf for your sin" (Lev 5:6 NRS). This sentence contains an important statement, in that atonement comes, not directly from God, but through a priest.

In the Book of Daniel, atonement comes from repentance since the sin was committed in Babylon which was too far away to allow an animal to be sacrificed in the Temple of Jerusalem: "But you take us! We come with a contrite heart and humble mind. As burnt offerings of rams and bulls, as thousands of fat lambs, so today our sacrifice should be valid to you and you give us atonement" (Dan 3:39 et seq).

The following passages prove that atonement came from God, through believing in, and loving Him: "But Hezekiah prayed for them, saying, "The good LORD pardon all who set their hearts to seek God, the LORD the God of their ancestors" (2Ch 30:18b-19a NRS); "For kindness to a father will not be forgotten, and will be credited to you against your sins; in the day of your distress it will be remembered in your favor; like frost in fair weather, your sins will melt away" (Sir 3:14-15 NRS).

This belief is attributed to Jesus in the Acts: "All the prophets testify about him that everyone who believes in him receives forgiveness of sins through his name" (Act 10:43 NRS).

A further example:

"I will rescue you from your people and from the Gentiles – to whom I am sending you to open their eyes so that they may turn from darkness to light and from the power of Satan to God, so that they may receive forgiveness of sins and a place among those who are sanctified by faith in me" (Act 26:17-18 NRS).

In light of the quotations from the Hebrew Bible, the Gospel reports on John the Baptist and his teachings about atonement can be seen as a continuation of this belief: "John the baptizer appeared in the wilderness, proclaiming a baptism of repentance for the forgiveness of sins. And people from the whole Judean countryside and all the people of Jerusalem were going out to him, and were baptized by him in the river Jordan, confessing their sins" (Mar 1:4-5 NRS). This is the first time that confession is mentioned as a prerequisite for the forgiveness of sin.

A further way of securing atonement, which the New Testament also adopted from Judaism, was to perform good deeds to atone for sins: "Therefore, O king, (Nebuchadnezzar) may my counsel be acceptable to you: atone for your sins with righteousness, and your iniquities with mercy to the oppressed, so that your prosperity may be prolonged" (Dan 4:27 NRS).

The same view is represented in the non-canonical Book of Tobit: "For alms-giving delivers from death and keeps you from going into the Darkness. Indeed, almsgiving, for all who practice it, is an excellent offering in the presence of the Most High" (Tob 4:10-11 NRS). And: "For almsgiving saves from death and purges away every sin. Those who give alms will enjoy a full life" (Tob 12:9 NRS).

The Gospel according to Matthew reflects this opinion voiced in Jewish scriptures that atonement can be obtained through the giving of alms as follows: "So whenever you give alms, do not sound a trumpet before you, as the hypocrites do in the synagogues and in the streets, so that they may be praised by others. Truly I tell you, they have received their reward. But when you give alms, do not let your left hand know what your right hand is doing, so that your alms may be done in secret; and your Father who sees in secret will reward you" (Mat 6:2-4 NRS).

The Gospel according to Matthew also emphasizes hospitality, which had become obligatory in Judaism following Abraham's example: "He looked up and saw three men standing near him. When he saw them, he ran from the tent entrance to meet them, and bowed down to the ground. He said, "My lord, if I find favor with you, do not pass by your servant. Let a little water be brought, and wash your feet, and rest yourselves under the tree. Let me bring a little bread, that you may refresh yourselves, and after that you may pass on – since you have come to your servant". So they said, "Do as you have said". And Abraham hastened into the tent to Sarah, and said, "Make ready quickly three measures of choice flour, knead it, and make cakes". Abraham ran to the herd, and took a calf, tender and good, and gave it to the servant, who hastened to prepare it. Then he took curds and milk and the calf that he had prepared, and set it before them; and he stood by them under the tree while they ate" (Gen 18:2-8 NRS).

Matthew writes: "Whoever welcomes you welcomes me, and whoever welcomes me welcomes the one who sent me. Whoever welcomes a prophet in the name of a prophet will receive a prophet's reward; and whoever welcomes a righteous person in the name of a righteous person will receive the reward of the righteous; and whoever gives even a cup of cold water to one of these little ones in the name of a disciple – truly I tell you, none of these will lose their reward" (Mat 10:40-42 NRS).

19. The sacrifice of Jesus as atonement

The sayings by the prophet Isaiah that have already been quoted deserve repetition at this point since they are important for the Christian teachings of atonement through the crucifixion of Jesus: "Yet it was the will of the LORD to crush him (the servant of God, see Isa 61:1-11 and 42:1-4/Mat 12:1-21) with pain. When you make his life an offering for sin, he shall see his offspring, and shall prolong his days; through him the will of the LORD shall prosper" (Isa 53:10 NRS). And: "He was despised and rejected by others; a man of suffering and acquainted with infirmity; and as one from whom others hide their faces he was despised, and we held him of no account. Surely he has borne our infirmities and carried our diseases; yet we accounted him stricken, struck down by God, and afflicted. But he was wounded for our transgressions, crushed for our iniquities; upon him was the punishment that made us whole, and by his bruises we are healed" (Isa 53:3-5 NRS).

It should be noted that the Hebrew word " חָלָל " can mean both "pierced" and "wounded". Both the Lutheran version of the Bible and the English King James version chose to translate " חָלָל " as "wounded" rather than pierced. This translation is supported by the Greek Septuagint, where " חָלָל " is translated as "ἐτραυματίσθη (Isa 53:5 BGT)". As such, this prophetic saying does not refer to Jesus' death, although Christian teachings relate the "Servant of God" to Jesus, since Matthew specifically states in his Gospel: "This was to fulfill what had been spoken through the prophet Isaiah (about Jesus): "Here is my servant, whom I have chosen, my beloved, with whom my soul is well pleased. I will put my Spirit upon him, and he will proclaim justice to the Gentiles. He will not wrangle or cry aloud, nor will anyone hear his voice in the streets. He will not break a bruised reed or quench a smoldering wick until he brings justice to victory. And in his name the Gentiles will hope" (Mat 12:17-21 NRS).

The Jewish doctrine explains the suffering of the Jewish people with the associated atonement of all other peoples.

The prophet Zechariah seems to have adopted the meaningful person of the "pierced one" or – in the Jewish view – the "wounded one" from the prophet Isaiah:

"And I will pour out a spirit of compassion and supplication on the house of David and the inhabitants of Jerusalem, so that, when they look on the one whom they have wounded, they shall mourn for him, as one mourns for an only child, and weep bitterly over him, as one weeps over a firstborn" (Zec 12:10 NRS). The translation in the New Revised Standard Version (1989) uses "pierced" instead of "wounded".

What is different about these statements is that someone is taking on someone else's sins in order to ensure their atonement:

"The righteous one, my servant, shall make many righteous, and he shall bear their iniquities. Therefore I will allot him a portion with the great, and he shall divide the spoil with the strong; because he poured out himself to death, and was numbered with the transgressors; yet he bore the sin of many, and made intercession for the transgressors" (Isa 53:11b-12 NRS).

Christianity linked the assumption of guilt and granting of atonement with the crucifixion of Jesus:

"...since all have sinned and fall short of the glory of God; they are now justified by his grace as a gift, through the redemption that is in Christ Jesus, whom God put forward as a sacrifice of atonement by his blood, effective through faith. He did this to show his righteousness, because in his divine forbearance he had passed over the sins previously committed" (Rom 3:23-25 NRS).

Equally:

"He destined us for adoption as his children through Jesus Christ, according to the good pleasure of his will, to the praise of his glorious grace that he freely bestowed on us in the Beloved. In him we have redemption through his blood, the forgiveness of our trespasses, according to the riches of his grace" (Eph 1:5-7 NRS).

And:

"He has rescued us from the power of darkness and transferred us into the kingdom of his beloved Son, in whom we have redemption, the forgiveness of sins... For in him all the fullness of God was pleased to dwell, and through him God was pleased to reconcile to himself all things, whether on earth or in heaven, by making peace through the blood of his cross" (Col 1:13-14 and 19-20 NRS).

The aforementioned sentences are evidence of the collective forgiveness of sins. The forgiveness of an individual's sins purely through the word of Jesus without the sinner having to explicitly do anything can be derived from the following sentence: "But so that you may know that the Son of Man has authority on earth to forgive sins" (Mat 9:6 NRS). (Similarly: Mar 2:10; Luk 5:24)

Although this passage does not mention that the sinner has to believe in Jesus to obtain atonement, this can be derived from other passages that have already been quoted.

The characteristic attributed to Jesus as the agent of God also allowed him to delegate the forgiveness of sins to his disciples with the help of the Holy Spirit: "Jesus said to them again "Peace be with you. As the Father has sent me, so I send you." When he had said this, he breathed on them and said to them "Receive the Holy Spirit. If you forgive the sins of any, they are forgiven them; if you retain the sins of any, they are retained" (Joh 20:21-23 NRS).

20. The forgiveness of sins through baptism

"And now why do you delay? Get up, be baptized, and have your sins washed away, calling on his name" (Act 22:16 NRS).

The baptismal phrase "baptizing them in the name of the Father and of the Son and of the Holy Spirit" (Mat 28:19b NRS) only features in Mat 28,19, but not in the narratives of baptism in the Acts and Paul's Letters. Passages that describe the act of baptism in more detail only use the baptismal phrase: "in the name of Jesus Christ" (Act 2:38 NRS). (Similarly: Acts 8:16; 10:48; 19:5; Rom 6:3 and Gal 3:27.) As such, Mat 28,19 may have been added at a later date. This baptismal phase from Mat 28,19 does, however, also appear in the Didache 7.1 (Greek: διδαχή), one of the earliest church orders of Christianity (c. 150-180, others claim 80-100 AD).

21. Individual peace

"Therefore, since we are justified by faith, we have peace with God through our Lord Jesus Christ" (Rom 5:1 NRS). This expression also appears in 2 Cor 13:11 and Rom 15:13.

The Hebrew Bible already featured the idea that the just "who love your law" live in peace with God. This expression is assumed to describe the modern term "peace of mind": "Great peace have those who love your law; nothing can make them stumble" (Psa 119:165 NRS).

22. The congregation of Jesus following his crucifixion, around 30 AD

The young congregation continued their untroubled lives following the crucifixion of Jesus: "They devoted themselves to the apostles' teaching and fellowship, to the breaking of bread and the prayers. Awe came upon everyone, because many wonders and signs were being done by the apostles. All who believed were together and had all things in common; they would sell their possessions and goods and distribute the proceeds to all, as any had need. Day by day, as they spent much time together in the temple, they broke bread at home and ate their food with glad and generous hearts, praising God and having the goodwill of all the people. And day by day the Lord added to their number those who were being saved" (Act 2:42-47 NRS).

Jews who did not believe that Jesus was the Messiah could not attend a church service at home since this was apparently linked to proskynesis according to the Letter of Paul to Philippians, 2,10: "Therefore God also highly exalted him and gave him the name that is above every name, so that at the name of Jesus **every knee should bend**, in heaven and on earth and under the earth, and every tongue should confess that Jesus Christ is Lord, to the glory of God the Father" (Phi 2:9-11 NRS). The services celebrated at home by the Christian congregations were, however, probably not standardized.

"it was in Antioch that the disciples were first called "Christians" (Act 11:26b NRS). This seems to have happened around 45 AD. Otherwise, the disciples of Jesus were seen as a sect within Judaism: "But this I (Paul) admit to you, that according to the Way, which they call a sect, I worship the God of our ancestors, believing everything laid down according to the law or written in the prophets" (Act 24:14 NRS). (Equally: Acts 28:16).

The expression "Nazarene" was aimed at Jesus (Mat 2:23; Acts 2:22; 3:6; 4:10; 6:14; 22:8; 26:9.). The expression "Nazarene sect" is only mentioned once in the New Testament, in Acts 24:5. This shows that at the time of writing the Acts, c. 80 - 90 AD, the disciples of Jesus were still seen as a sect and had not yet segregated from Judaism. This claim cannot, however, be generalized since it is possible that a different situation prevailed in certain places.

23. The Gentiles

Although Paul was primarily active in converting the heathens to Christianity and managed to get the Apostolic Council (Acts chap. 15,) to agree to baptism without prior circumcision, it was Peter who was first linked to the conversion of the Gentiles in the Acts:

"While Peter was still speaking, the Holy Spirit fell upon all who heard the word. The circumcised believers who had come with Peter were astounded that the gift of the Holy Spirit had been poured out even on the Gentiles, for they heard them speaking in tongues and extolling God. Then Peter said, "Can anyone withhold the water for baptizing these people who have received the Holy Spirit just as we have?" So he ordered them to be baptized in the name of Jesus Christ" (Act 10:44-48a NRS).

Peter is also named in the Acts as being the person responsible for Christians not adhering to Jewish food laws:

"He saw the heaven opened and something like a large sheet coming down, being lowered to the ground by its four corners. In it were all kinds of four-footed creatures and reptiles and birds of the air. Then he heard a voice saying "Get up, Peter; kill and eat." But Peter said, "By no means, Lord; for I have never eaten anything that is profane or unclean." The voice said to him again, a second time, "What God has made clean, you must not call profane." This happened three times, and the thing was suddenly taken up to heaven" (Act 10:13-16).

The Acts also narrate that it was Peter who spoke the decisive words at the Apostolic Council in Jerusalem:

"After there had been much debate, Peter stood up and said to them "My brothers, you know that in the early days God made a choice among you, that I should be the one through whom the Gentiles would hear the message of the good news and become believers. And God, who knows the human heart, testified to them by giving them the Holy Spirit, just as he did to us; and in cleansing their hearts by faith he has made no distinction between them and us. Now therefore why are you putting God to the test by placing on the neck of the disciples a yoke that neither our ancestors nor we have been able to bear? On the contrary, we believe that we will be saved through the grace of the Lord Jesus, just as they will" (Act 15:7-11 NRS).

Paul narrates this in his Letter to the Galatians which was, however, written some thirty years before the Acts of the Apostles. His narrative paints a different picture of the events at the Apostolic Council:

"... we did not submit to them even for a moment, so that the truth of the gospel might always remain with you. And from those who were supposed to be acknowledged leaders, what they actually were makes no difference to me; God shows no partiality, – those leaders contributed nothing to me. On the contrary, when they saw that I had been entrusted with the gospel for the uncircumcised, just as Peter had been entrusted with the gospel for the circumcised, for he who worked through Peter making him an apostle to the circumcised also worked through me in sending me to the Gentiles, and when James and Cephas and John, who were acknowledged pillars, recognized the grace that had been given to me, they gave to Barnabas and me the right hand of fellowship, agreeing that we should go to the Gentiles and they to the circumcised. They asked only one thing, that we remember the poor, which was actually what I was eager to do" (Gal 2:5-10 NRS).

The role that Paul had in convening the Apostolic Council was also played down in the Acts of the Apostles:

"Then certain individuals came down from Judea and were teaching the brothers "Unless you are circumcised according to the custom of Moses, you cannot be saved." And after Paul and Barnabas had no small dissension and debate with them, Paul and Barnabas and some of the others were appointed to go up to Jerusalem to discuss this question with the apostles and the elders" (Act 15:1-2 NRS).

It would seem as though Christians placed more importance on Peter as the successor charged by Jesus than on Paul, although it was Paul who succeeded in having the Jewish laws abolished for Gentiles against the will of the traditionally minded Jewish Christians who observed the Jewish laws.

The aforementioned quotation from the Acts of the Apostles 15:1 et seq only relates to circumcision but as the following quotation will show, the meeting of the Apostles also addressed the issue of food laws: "Therefore I (Jacobus) have reached the decision that we should not trouble those Gentiles who are turning to God, but we should write to them to abstain only from things polluted by idols and from fornication and from whatever has been strangled and from blood" (Act 15:19-20 NRS).

The dispute in Jerusalem that is mentioned in chap. 15 is deemed to have been the first Apostolic Council (45 - 46 or 48 - 49 AD); the resolution adopted by the Council allowed Gentiles to be baptized without committing to observe Jewish laws. This caused tension, not only with the Jews but also with the Jewish Christians.

24. Meat sacrificed to idols

"But when Cephas came to Antioch, I opposed him to his face, because he stood self-condemned; for until certain people came from James, he used to eat with the Gentiles. But after they came, he drew back and kept himself separate for fear of the circumcision faction. And the other Jews joined him in this hypocrisy, so that even Barnabas was led astray by their hypocrisy. But when I saw that they were not acting consistently with the truth of the gospel, I said to Cephas before them all "If you, though a Jew, live like a Gentile and not like a Jew, how can you compel the Gentiles to live like Jews?" We ourselves are Jews by birth and not Gentile sinners; yet we know that a person is justified not by the works of the law but through faith in Jesus Christ" (Gal 2:11-16a NRS).

It is questionable whether the Jews had any additional food restrictions by law, apart from those that the Apostolic Council had committed the gentile Christians to observe. This conflict seems to have arisen because Paul did not accept the commitments imposed by the Apostolic Council, as narrated in the Acts, which is why the gentile Christians did not adhere to them.

Towards the end of his life, Paul seems to have become more conciliatory. The following sentence can only refer to food that the Apostolic Council had forbidden: if Jewish Christians also observed the food laws that extended beyond this resolution, they would not have aroused any offence among the gentile Christians. As such, the words can only relate to gentile Christians who ate food that was offensive to Jewish Christians.

"Do not, for the sake of food, destroy the work of God. Everything is indeed clean, but it is wrong for you to make others fall by what you eat; it is good not to eat meat or drink wine or do anything that makes your brother or sister stumble. The faith that you have, have as your own conviction before God. Blessed are those who have no reason to condemn themselves because of what they approve. But those who have doubts are condemned if they eat, because the do not act from faith; for whatever does not proceed from faith is sin" (Rom 14:20-23 NRS).

The following sentence from Revelation is also aimed at those Christians who ate sacrificial meat, which, it seemed, they were tempted to do because the meat was cheaper: "... so that they would eat food sacrificed to idols and practice fornication" (Rev 2:14b NRS).

The following passage from a letter is further proof that Paul did not accept the food restrictions that were decreed by the Apostolic Council:

"If an unbeliever invites you to a meal and you are disposed to go, eat whatever is set before you without raising any question on the ground of conscience. But if someone says to you 'This has been offered in sacrifice,' then do not eat it, out of consideration for the one who informed you, and for the sake of conscience – I mean the other's conscience, not your own. For why should my liberty be subject to the judgment of someone else's conscience? If I partake with thankfulness, why should I be denounced because of that for which I give thanks? So, whether you eat or drink, or whatever you do, do everything for the glory of God. Give no offense to Jews or to Greeks or to the church of God" (1Co 10:27-32 NRS).

By saying the following, Paul denies the existence of anything such as meat sacrificed to idols:

"Hence, as to the eating of food offered to idols, we know that "no idol in the world really exists," and that "there is no God but one". Indeed, even though there may be so-called gods in heaven or on earth – as in fact there are many gods and many lords – yet for us there is one God, the Father" (1Cor 8,4 et seqq).

25. Circumcision

Paul seems to have tolerated the circumcision of Jewish Christians at first, as illustrated by the following sentences:

"Circumcision indeed is of value if you obey the law; but if you break the law, your circumcision has become uncircumcision. So, if those who are uncircumcised keep the requirements of the law, will not their uncircumcision be regarded as circumcision? Then those who are physically uncircumcised but keep the law will condemn you that have the written code and circumcision but break the law. For a person is not a Jew who is one outwardly, nor is true circumcision something external and physical. Rather, a person is a Jew who is one inwardly, and real circumcision is a matter of the heart – it is spiritual and not literal. Such a person receives praise not from others but from God" (Rom 2:25-29 NRS).

"Then what advantage has the Jew? Or what is the value of circumcision? Much, in every way. For in the first place the Jews were entrusted with the oracles of God. What if some were unfaithful? Will their faithlessness nullify the faithfulness of God? By no means! Although everyone is a liar, let God be proved true, as it is written, "So that you may be justified in your words, and prevail in your judging" (Rom 3:1-4 NRS).

The following saying by Paul further deepened the trench between Gentile Christians and Jewish Christians. The Jewish Christians adhered to Jewish laws but believed that Jesus was the Messiah:

"For freedom Christ has set us free. Stand firm, therefore, and do not submit again to a yoke of slavery. Listen! I, Paul, am telling you that if you let yourselves be circumcised, Christ will be of no benefit to you. Once again I testify to every man who lets himself be circumcised that he is obliged to obey the entire law. You who want to be justified by the law have cut yourselves off from Christ; you have fallen away from grace. For through the Spirit, by faith, we eagerly wait for the hope of righteousness. For in Christ Jesus neither circumcision nor uncircumcision counts for anything; the only thing that counts is faith working through love" (Gal 5:1-6 NRS).

This saying by Paul was extremely important for future developments since – as a result – Jewish Christians, who existed up to at least the 7th century AD, were seen by the Gentile majority as not being part of Christianity. They were called "Judaizers". As we will see later on, they were later accused of being heretics and had to suffer the consequences accordingly.

As can be seen from the following sentence, circumcision was understood as a disavowal of Christianity:

"But my friends, why am I still being persecuted if I am still preaching circumcision? In that case the offense of the cross has been removed" (Gal 5:11 NRS). In the light of accusations that he opposed circumcision, it would seem that Paul had to prove himself to be an orthodox Jew so as not to unsettle the Jewish Christians in their faith:

"Then they said to him, "You see, brother, how many thousands of believers there are among the Jews, and they are all zealous for the law. They have been told about you that you teach all the Jews living among the Gentiles to forsake Moses, and that you tell them not to circumcise their children or observe the customs. What then is to be done? They will certainly hear that you have come. So do what we tell you. We have four men who are under a vow. Join these men, go through the rite of purification with them, and pay for the shaving of their heads. Thus all will know that there is nothing in what they have been told about you, but that you yourself observe and guard the law" (Act 21:20-24NRS).

Paul took the advice:

"Then Paul took the men, and the next day, having purified himself, he entered the temple with them, making public the completion of the days of purification when the sacrifice would be made for each of them" (Act21:26 NRS). This purification rite that Paul underwent is the Nasirat: This purification rite is described in Numeri chap. 6 of the Torah. The first verses read as follows: "The LORD spoke to Moses, saying: "Speak to the Israelites and say to them: When either men or women make a special vow, the vow of a nazirite, to separate themselves to the LORD..." (Num 6:1-2 NRS).

There were other occasions on which Paul professed to be an orthodox Jew:

"Brothers and fathers, listen to the defense that I now make before you." When they heard him addressing them in Hebrew, they became even more quiet. Then he said: "I am a Jew, born in Tarsus in Cilicia, but brought up in this city at the feet of Gamaliel, educated strictly according to our ancestral law, being zealous for God, just as all of you are today" (Act 22:1-3 NRS).

26. The conflicts within the Christian community

The above shows that the various Christian congregations held different views about the teachings of Jesus. Paul also complained about this divergence:

"For it has been reported to me by Chloe's people that there are quarrels among you, my brothers and sisters. What I mean is that each of you says "I belong to Paul", or "I belong to Apollos", or "I belong to Cephas", or "I belong to Christ". "Has Christ been divided? Was Paul crucified for you? Or were you baptized in the name of Paul?" (1Co 1:11-13 NRS). John the Evangelist, who is usually attributed with writing the First Letter of John, describes these contradictions as deeds of the anti-Christ:

"Children, it is the last hour! As you have heard that antichrist is coming, so now many antichrists have come. From this we know that it is the last hour. They went out from us, but they did not belong to us; for if they had belonged to us, they would have remained with us. But by going out they made it plain that none of them belongs to us" (1Jo 2:18-19 NRS).

"Many deceivers have gone out into the world, those who do not confess that Jesus Christ has come in the flesh; any such person is the deceiver and the antichrist!" (2Jo 1:7 NRS).

As a result of the inner-Christian conflicts, it was not until towards the end of the second century that a more or less uniform view of the "orthodox scriptures about Jesus" that were summarized in the Gospels emerged among the leading men of the church. In addition to the four canonical Gospels, the Synod in Rome in 382 AD acknowledged the orthodoxy, of the Acts of the Apostles, 23 Letters to Christian congregations and one apocalypse – the Revelation of John. This marked the approval of the canon as we know it today.

A series of extra-canonical texts and texts by the church fathers against the "heresies", especially of Irenaeus, show that there were some substantially contradictory theologian views circulating in Christianity between the 2nd and 4th centuries. The various Councils attempted to establish a clear consistent theological view. However, the fractions that were defeated in such decisions by the Council then often went off and set up their own independent churches. One important segregation that still exists to this day was the so-called East-West Schism in 1054, from which the Roman Catholic church and the Eastern Orthodox churches under the honorary primacy of the Patriarch of Constantinople emerged. Further schisms occurred in the 16th century, resulting in the emergence of the various protestant faiths.

27. The disassociation of the Jews from the Jewish Christians

Four passages in the Gospels according to Luke and John narrate the ejection of Jewish Christians by Jews from the synagogue. Since the latter was written about 20 years after the Gospel according to Luke but was only circulated in a limited area in Jerusalem and Asia Minor, it is probable that this "ejection" of believers of Jesus from synagogues only took place over a limited period and in a limited area:

"Blessed are you when people hate you, and when they exclude you, revile you, and defame you on account of the Son of Man" (Luk 6:22 NRS).

His parents said this because they were afraid of the Jews; for the Jews had already agreed that anyone who confessed Jesus to be the Messiah would be put out of the synagogue" (Joh 9:22 NRS).

"Nevertheless many, even of the authorities, believed in him. But because of the Pharisees they did not confess it, for fear that they would be put out of the synagogue; for they loved human glory more than the glory that comes from God" (Joh 12:42-43 NRS).

"They will put you out of the synagogues. Indeed, an hour is coming when those who kill you will think that by doing so they are offering worship to God. And they will do this because they have not known the Father or me" (Joh 16:2-3 NRS).

In earlier times, this disassociation was attributed to the addition of a new paragraph to the Amidah, the central prayer that has to be repeated three times a day, although the quotations above refer to total exclusion (cherem) rather than to a prayer. This addition to the Amidah was apparently introduced by the Rabbi Gamaliel around 90 AD in Yavne:

"For slanderers let there be no hope, and let all wickedness instantly perish. May all Thy enemies be quickly cut off; and as for the malicious, swiftly uproot, break, cast down, and subdue quickly in our day. Blessed art Thou, Lord, who breaks the power of His enemies and subdues the malicious."

This theory is no longer sustainable in light of the recent research findings by Günter Stemberger. The first written reference to this addition does not appear until quite some time after 90 AD, in the 4th century if not even later, in the Palestinian Talmud. It mentions the Minim (probably heretics), against whom this saying was apparently directed. Stemberger rightly asks when such a saying was introduced and, if directed against the Christians, why were they not named expressis verbis. He believes that there is little likelihood that this text was directed against the believers of Jesus since Christianity had not assumed a level of importance in 90 AD Palestine that would have justified such an addition. Thirdly, Stemberger doubts that the people surrounding Rabbi Gamaliel would have exerted sufficient influence on the Jewish congregations to secure the generalized application of such a new attitude. What is more likely is that certain Jewish congregations in the Diaspora felt threatened by Christianization and therefore resolved to adopt a measure, such as the introduction of a prayer directed against Christians, to prevent any infiltration by Christians. (Stemberger, The birkat haminim and the separation of Christians and Jews, will be published shortly)

The flogging of the believers of Jesus, as narrated in 2 Cor 11:25; Mat 10:17; 23:34; Acts 5:40 also seems to have been locally contained over a limited period of time since it is no longer mentioned in later sources.

This raises the question as to how credible the following confession by Paul, which was directed at Jewish Christians, really is. It could equally be that these words were not spoken by him but were added at a later date: "To my shame, I must say, we were too weak for that! But whatever anyone dares to boast of – I am speaking as a fool – I also dare to boast of that. Are they Hebrews? So am I. Are they Israelites? So am I. Are they descendants of Abraham? So am I. Are they ministers of Christ? I am talking like a madman – I am a better one: with far greater labors, far more imprisonments, with countless floggings, and often near death. Five times I have received from the Jews the forty lashes minus one. Three times I was beaten with rods. Once I received a stoning" (2Co 11:21-25 NRS). Stoning such as was practiced back then ended when the person being stoned was dead. For example: "While they were stoning Stephen, he prayed, "Lord Jesus, receive my spirit." Then he knelt down and cried out in a loud voice, "Lord, do not hold this sin against them." When he had said this, he died" (Act 7:59-60 NRS).

The descriptions used by Paul in his speech are also somewhat strange, since the expressions "Hebrews", "Israelites", "descendants of Abraham" and "Jews" are actually synonymous.

It would seem that "flogging" was more a symbolic act of punishment, as can be derived from the narrative in Act 5:40 et seqq: "... and when they (the members of the High Council) had called in the apostles, they had them flogged. Then they ordered them not to speak in the name of Jesus, and let them go. As they left the council, they rejoiced that they were considered worthy to suffer dishonor for the sake of the name. And every day in the temple and at home they did not cease to teach and proclaim Jesus as the Messiah."

The punishment of thirty-nine lashes derives from Deu 25:1 et seqq, where it is written: "Suppose two persons have a dispute and enter into litigation, and the judges decide between them, declaring one to be in the right and the other to be in the wrong. If the one in the wrong deserves to be flogged, the judge shall make that person lie down and be beaten in his presence with the number of lashes proportionate to the offense. Forty lashes may be given but not more; if more lashes than these are given, your neighbor will be degraded in your sight" (Deu 25:1 et seqq).

The Rabbis decided (M.Mak, 3:11) to reduce this number by one in order to avoid the danger, when giving forty lashes, of miscounting and flogging the guilty party forty-one times which would have constituted a violation of biblical law. The Mishnah were not written until around 220 AD. Both here and in many other places, the New Testament surprisingly recorded Jewish laws in writing much earlier than the Jewish scriptures.

Justin is the only person in the second century AD to refer to the exclusion of believers of Jesus from the synagogue by cursing them there: "for you have slain the Just One, and His prophets before Him; and now you reject those who hope in Him, and in Him who sent Him—God the Almighty and Maker of all things— cursing in your synagogues those that believe in Christ" (Dialogue with Trypho the Jew, 16:4; similarly: 93:4; 95:4; 96:2; 108:3; 123:6; 133:6; 137:2).

The New Testament repeatedly mentions the accusation that prophets were killed by the ancestors of the Jews: "Thus you testify against yourselves that you are descendants of those who murdered the prophets" (Mat 23:31 NRS). Similarly: Luk 13:34, Act 7:52, Rom 11:3, probably with reference to 1 Kings 19:10: "He answered, "I have been very zealous for the LORD, the God of hosts; for the Israelites have forsaken your covenant, thrown down your altars, and killed your prophets with the sword. I alone am left, and they are seeking my life, to take it away" (1Ki 19:10 NRS).

Epiphanius of Salamis, around 315 – 403 AD, and Hieronymus, 347 - 420 AD, claimed that the Jews cursed the "Nazarenes" three times a day in their prayers.[42]

Given the lack of standardization in synagogue services, such prayers might well have initially been local before ultimately being adopted by the majority of synagogues over time. As demonstrated by the prayer text quoted above, however, they were directed against the Minim (heretics) and not the Christians.

The passages that bear witness to the presence of "God fearers" in the synagogue, by contrast, are much clearer, indicating that Gentiles who were interested in the Jewish faith but not ready to convert, possibly because of the circumcision and food laws, could freely attend a service at a synagogue:"So Paul stood up and with a gesture began to speak: "You Israelites, and others who fear God, listen" (Act 13:16 NRS). And:

"My brothers, you descendants of Abraham's family, and others who fear God" (Act 13:26a NRS). (Equally: Act 17:4 and 17:17).

Presumably, a solution had to be found for the "God fearing" community that was also acceptable to the Jews as they otherwise would not have been able to pray together nor would any resulting social interaction with the "Infidels" have been possible.

The Jewish "Book of Jubilees" which dates back to the 2nd century BC already refer to the Noachide Commandments that must be observed by non-Jews if they are to enjoy the same positive expectations for the future as orthodox Jews.

"And in the twenty-eighth jubilee Noah began to enjoin upon his sons' sons the ordinances and commandments, and all the judgments that he knew, and he exhorted his sons to observe righteousness, and to cover the shame of their flesh, and to bless their Creator, and honor father and mother, and love their neighbor, and guard their souls from fornication and uncleanness and all iniquity" (7:20).

The Sybilline Oracles (Lat.: *Oracula Sibyllina*) probably pursued the same objectives in IV, 24-42 and especially 37-42. These oracles are a collection of allegedly prophetic writings that were collated in the 6th century and drawn from Jewish, Christian and heathen sources between 150 BC and 300 AD. Book IV, 37-42 says: "... and they will look To the great glory of one God and not Commit presumptuous murder nor dispose Of stolen gain, which things most horrid are; Nor shameful longing for another's bed Have they, nor vile and hateful lust of males."[43] The Book as we know it today was written by a Jewish author between 80 and 90 AD.

Judaism defined seven laws as the Noachide Commandments (or Seven Laws of Noah) that were applicable to all mankind. Non-Jews who complied with the laws could "participate in the coming world" as "righteous people" (Zaddik), which is why Judaism does not teach the necessity of converting people of other faiths. On the contrary, a Rabbi is obligated to thrice reject a person who wants to convert to Judaism and to make sure that the person is aware of the obligations that face converts, none of which raise their chances of redemption.

The Noachide Laws cover: The prohibition of idolatry, the prohibition of blasphemy, the establishment of law courts, the prohibition of murder, the prohibition of adultery, the prohibition of theft and the prohibition of eating flesh taken from an animal while it is still alive. These laws were included in the Talmud in bSanh 56b.[44]

Several grave inscriptions up to the 5th century that were found in Rome bear witness to the existence of this group of "God fearers".[45]

28. The split between Jewish Christians and Judaism

As narrated in the Gospel according to John, Christians were "ejected" from the synagogue in some places, i.e. they were excluded from the community.

It is not even certain whether this exclusion from the community only applied to the Gentile Christians as they did not observe the Jewish laws. Flogging and "ejection" do not seem have been the rule between Jews and Jewish Christians, since Paul and his successors accepted that Jewish Christians followed the Jewish laws even as late as 50 - 80 AD[46]:

"Welcome those who are weak in faith, but not for the purpose of quarreling over opinions. Some believe in eating anything, while the weak eat only vegetables. Those who eat must not despise those who abstain, and those who abstain must not pass judgment on those who eat; for God has welcomed them. Who are you to pass judgment on servants of another? It is before their own lord that they stand or fall. And they will be upheld, for the Lord is able to make them stand. Some judge one day to be better than another, while others judge all days to be alike. Let all be fully convinced in their own minds. Those who observe the day, observe it in honor of the Lord. Also those who eat, eat in honor of the Lord, since they give thanks to God; while those who abstain, abstain in honor of the Lord and give thanks to God" (Rom 14:1-6 NRS).

Equally: "Therefore do not let anyone condemn you in matters of food and drink or of observing festivals, new moons, or sabbaths" (Col 2:16 NRS).

A further separation away from Judaism occurred when the "Day of the Lord" was moved from Saturday to Sunday. This was a gradual process that occurred between the 2nd and 4th centuries AD. Initially, the Christians celebrated their day on the Sunday without questioning the Saturday as the rightful Sabbath. The Bible says: "On the first day of the week (Sunday), when we met to break bread" (Act 20:7 NRS).

The disassociation of the Jewish Christians from the Jews seems to have been subject to different processes in different places, since the accusations of secession of Jewish Christians from Judaism were not voiced by all of the church fathers.

In his Homilies on Leviticus 5,8 (GCS 6.349.4 et seq), Origen claims that people would come to his (Sunday) sermons who obviously had been to the synagogue the day before. It therefore seems that these Jews who felt drawn towards Christianity did not feel that the "birkat ha-minim" applied to them – provided this prayer existed at that time. Origen also mentions that Jesus was cursed and vilified by Jews. (Hom. Jer. X,8,2; XIX,12,31; Hom. Ps. 27, II,8). Since Origen was closely linked to the Rabbis, his knowledge of Jewish service was excellent. It is therefore unlikely that he would not have made reference to this passage about the prayer in the birkat ha-minim if it had been commonplace in Caesarea when mentioning any cursing of Christians.[47]

29. The Jewish Christian community

Particular attention was paid to the Jewish Christians who observed the laws of Judaism in the Epistle of Ignatius to the Magnesians (around the middle of the 2nd century AD):[48]

"It is absurd to profess Christ Jesus, and to Judaize. For Christianity did not merge into Judaism, but Judaism into Christianity, that so every tongue which believeth might be gathered together to God" (Epistle to the Magnesians 10:3).

Ignatius adds a warning:

"Lay aside, therefore, the evil, the old, the corrupt leaven (1 Cor 1,7) and be ye changed into the new leaven of grace. Abide in Christ, that the enemy may not have dominion over you. It is absurd to speak of Jesus Christ with the tongue, and to cherish in the mind a Judaism which has now come to an end. For where there is Christianity there cannot be Judaism. For Christ is one, in whom every nation that believes, and every tongue that confesses, is gathered unto God" (Epistle to the Magnesians 10:8-10).

Ignatius also seems to have received news of similar circumstances prevailing in Philadelphia, which is why he wrote to the Christian congregation there: "But if any one preach Judaism unto you, listen not to him. For it is better to hearken to Christian doctrine from a man who has been circumcised, than to Judaism from one uncircumcised" (Epistle to the Ephesians 6,1).

The Epistle to Diognetus, 2nd century AD, contains the following relevant sections: In chapters 3 and 4, the Jews are accused of practicing an incomprehensible and unnatural faith. These chapters are probably directed at Jewish Christians. The chapters narrate the following:

They still render homage to a superstition, with the addition of a warning that

Their sacrificial rites were also meaningless, and

Their other religious practices were just as objectionable.

On 7 March 321 AD, Emperor Constantine I declared Sunday as the official day of rest; markets were forbidden and the public offices closed on this day (CJ 3.12.2). No restrictions were imposed, however, on working the land, which was the occupation of the large majority of the population. This regulation made it harder for Jews and Jewish Christians to observe the laws of the Sabbath. The Sabbath had never been a day of rest in the Roman Empire anyway, even before this declaration; it could only be practiced by self-employed Jews.

The following chapters from the resolution adopted by the Synod of Laodicea, in Phrygia Pacatiana, 364 AD, are relevant for Judaizing Christians:

Cn. 16 "On the reading on the Sabbath": The Gospels are to be read on the Sabbath, together with the other writings. ("other writings" probably refer to the scriptures summarized in the New Testament, although they were not canonized until 382 AD).

Cn. 29: Christians must not judaize by resting on the Sabbath, but must work on that day, rather honoring the Lord's Day ... But if any shall be found to be judaizers, let them be anathema from Christ.

Cn. 37: It is not lawful to receive portions sent from the feasts of Jews or heretics, nor to feast together with them.[49]

As Chrysostomos writes in his work "Adversus Judaeos", he preached eight sermons against the Jews in Antioch in 386/7 AD, which were, however, basically directed against Judaizing Christians:

4.3,5. "What, then, are the questions? I will ask each one who is sick with this disease: Are you a Christian? Why, then, this zeal for Jewish practices? Are you a Jew? Why then, are you making trouble for the Church? ... How, then, do you expect to be saved by defecting to that unlawful way of life?"

4.3.6. "The difference between the Jews and us is not a small one, is it? Is the dispute between us over ordinary, everyday matters, so that you think the two religions are really one and the same? Why are you mixing what cannot be mixed? They crucified the Christ whom you adore as God. Do you see how great the difference is? How is it, then, that you keep running to those who slew Christ when you say that you worship him whom they crucified? You do not think, do you, that I am the one who brings up the law on which these charges are based, nor that I make up the form which the accusation takes? Does not the Scripture treat the Jews in this way?"

The following resolution was adopted by the Synod of Carthage in 398 AD:

Cn. 89: "....A follower of Jewish superstitions and Jewish holidays, should be excluded from the community of the church".

In his work "Quaestiones adversus Iudaeos ac ceteros infideles", which dates from around 560, Isidore of Seville, † 4 April 636, also attacked Judaizing Christians.

Fig. 3. Mosaics on the west wall of the Basilica of Santa Sabina in Rome before 430 AD.

Writings may well also have existed that were not hostile to Judaizing Christians but which were later destroyed in the course of Christian censorship. Otherwise, the mosaic in Sta. Sabina, before 430 AD, could not have depicted two women, each entitled "Ecclesia ex gentibus" and "Ecclesia ex circumcisione". Each woman holds an open book with an ostensibly different font. This could imply that the mosaic is trying to depict the "Ecclesia ex circumcisione" holding the Old Testament in Hebrew, and the "Ecclesia ex gentibus" holding the New Testament in Latin or Greek. If these Jewish Christians, depicted in this mosaic by "Ecclesia ex circumcisione" as part of the church, had not upheld their Jewish tradition over the course of generations and, in addition, had been able to read Hebrew, then they would surely have forgotten that they descended from the Israclites, and the depiction of the "two parts of the church" would have had no meaning.

Fig. 4. The mosaic in the apse of Sta. Pudenziana in Rome, late 4th century AD

A mosaic dating from the late 4th century AD has survived in the basilica of Sta. Pudenziana, also in Rome, which depicts two women offering wreaths to the apostles Peter (on the right) and Paul (on the left) This depiction is presumably also meant to symbolize that part of the church congregation descended from Jews. The woman offering the wreath to Peter is probably meant to symbolize Ecclesia ex circumcisione.

Towards the end of the 4th century AD, the fathers of the church tried to strengthen its inner unity, which was being threatened by Arianism and other heresies. This may have taken the dispute between Gentiles and Jewish Christians out of the spotlight. The unity of the church needed to be emphasized in order to resolve the dispute, which is why the equal standing of these two origins of the church was emphasized in its iconography. There does not, at least, seem to be any other explanation for the sudden appearance of these depictions since these two women only featured in church mosaics for a couple of decades.

Several mosaics dating from the 5th and 6th centuries and found in Jordan depict two bulls to the left and right of a burning altar, for which there is no simple explanation. Researcher Michele Piccirillo writes: "The inclusion of a quotation from Psalm 51 ("Then they shall lay calves upon Your altar"), in the composition of two bulls on either side of a burning altar found in both the mosaics makes the scene an allegory of sacrifice".[50]

Fig. 5. Mosaic in the Church of Sts. Lot and Procopius on Mount Nobo, Jordan, 7th century AD

The author is grateful for Piccirillo's reference to these words from Psalm 51:21b in the Byzantine mass rite: In the "Divine Liturgy of Saint John Chrysostom" the priest thrice waves incense over the "gifts", repeats this three times and "and then bulls are sacrificed on Your altar".[51] The verse in Psalm 51:18 et seq reads as follows: "Do good to Zion in your good pleasure; rebuild the walls of Jerusalem, then you will delight in right sacrifices, in burnt offerings and whole burnt offerings; then bulls will be offered on your altar".

If this verse was an attempt at allegorizing the Eucharist, it is strange that the rebuilding of Jerusalem was used in comparison. The "Divine Liturgy" mentioned above was not written by John Chrysostom, although it was attributed to him.

Another mosaic depicting the same image can be found close by, also on Mount Nebo:

Fig. 6. Mosaic in the Theotokos Chapel in the Basilica of Moses on Mount Nebo

I agree with Father Piccirillo that these mosaics are allegorical. Such Christian allegories usually relate to the scheme of promise and fulfillment. The question is: Which promise is meant? Is the promise the Eucharist or the rebuilding of Zion and its shrine? Christian iconography always focuses on fulfillment. Apart from a few exceptions, a sequence of images first depicts the promise, but then also the fulfillment. The mosaics in this case seem to focus on fulfillment. It would not be easily explainable that the bulls are slaughtered in heaven where, according to Jewish belief, the shrine is located that serves as the role model for earthly shrines.

The following section taken from the previous mosaic shows the expected shrine with the burning altar.

Fig. 7. Mosaic in the Theotokos Chapel in the Basilica of Moses on Mount Nebo, Jordan, early 6th century AD, section: the shrine

The layout of the mosaics could point to a judaizing Christian sect in the 5th and 6th centuries that anticipated the rebuilding of the temple. This expectation and the related sacrificial animals would contradict the Christian belief sacrificial offerings in the temple had been made obsolete by Jesus' sacrifice (see, for example, Heb 9:26 et seqq).

30. Is Christianity the true Israel?

In Christian doctrine, statements from the Hebrew Bible were interpreted in relation to the New Testament. As such, Christians believed that Judaism had lost its the theological foundation since the Hebrew Bible no longer possessed any value of its own. It was seen only as a "promise" that found its "fulfillment" in the New Testament.

The interpretation of the statements in the Hebrew Bible relative to the New Testament was known as "typology", and church scholars outdid each other in finding such typologies. Typology formed a link between the Hebrew Bible and the New Testament and was seen as proof that Christianity embodied "true Judaism". This was also highlighted by the term "Late Judaism" used for Judaism, for whose existence there was no theological justification since the Hebrew Bible is only comprehensible and valid from the perspective of the New Testament. The Hebrew Bible was seen to only bear witness to the rightness of the Christian teachings. The Christians placed all the more value on this witness because it came from their adversaries, the Jews.

Paul already makes use of such typologies, for example in Gal 4:22-25: "For it is written that Abraham had two sons, one by a slave woman and the other by a free woman. One, the child of the slave, was born according to the flesh; the other, the child of the free woman, was born through the promise. Now this is an allegory: these women are two covenants. One woman, in fact, is Hagar, from Mount Sinai, bearing children for slavery. Now Hagar is Mount Sinai in Arabia and corresponds to the present Jerusalem, for she is in slavery with her children. But the other woman corresponds to the Jerusalem above; she is free, and she is our mother" (Gal 4:22-26 NRS).

One component of typology, as already mentioned above, is the exegeses which claim that Christianity is the true Israel, unlike Judaism, which had erred from the path of God. One example of this is a quotation from Paul's Letter, Rom 9:6-9: "It is not as though the word of God had failed. For not all Israelites truly belong to Israel, and not all of Abraham's children are his true descendants; but it is through Isaac that descendants shall be named for you. This means that it is not the children of the flesh who are the children of God, but the children of the promise are counted as descendants. For this is what the promise said, "About this time I will return and Sarah shall have a son".

In the following example, Paul shows how Israel was moved away from the roots of true Judaism and Christianity planted in the latter's place:

"If the part of the dough offered as first fruits is holy, then the whole batch is holy; and if the root is holy, then the branches also are holy. But if some of the branches were broken off, and you, a wild olive shoot, were grafted in their place to share the rich root of the olive tree, do not boast over the branches. If you do boast, remember that it is not you that support the root, but the root that supports you" (Rom 11:16-18 NRS).

The Gospels also represent the Hebrew Bible as only being comprehensible through the words of Jesus:

"Then he (Jesus) said to them, "These are my words that I spoke to you while I was still with you – that everything written about me in the law of Moses, the prophets, and the psalms must be fulfilled. Then he opened their minds to understand the scriptures" (Luk 24:44-45NRS).

And:

"You search the scriptures because you think that in them you have eternal life; and it is they that testify on my behalf. Yet you refuse to come to me to have life.... If you believed Moses, you would believe me, for he wrote about me. But if you do not believe what he wrote, how will you believe what I say?" (Joh 5:39-40 and 46-47 NRS).

The Gospels also emphasize that the Jews will no longer be part of the calling of Israel, but that they will be replaced by other nations that shall then represent the true Israel: "There will be weeping and gnashing of teeth when you see Abraham and Isaac and Jacob and all the prophets in the kingdom of God, and you yourselves thrown out. Then people will come from east and west, from north and south, and will eat in the kingdom of God" (Luk 13:28-29 NRS).

Equally:

I (Jesus) tell you, many will come from east and west and will eat with Abraham and Isaac and Jacob in the kingdom of heaven, while the heirs of the kingdom will be thrown into the outer darkness, where there will be weeping and gnashing of teeth" (Mat 8:11 et seq).

Subsequent church scholars perpetuated this view professed in the New Testament that Christianity represented the "true Israel". This is shown, for example, by the following quotation from the middle of the 2nd century AD:

"For the true spiritual Israel, and descendants of Judah, Jacob, Isaac, and Abraham, who in uncircumcision was approved of and blessed by God on account of his faith, and called the father of many nations, are we who have been led to God through this crucified Christ" (Dialogue of Justin, Philosopher and Martyr, with Trypho, a Jew 11,5).

One typology by Tertullian (c.150 - c. 230) had disastrous consequences for Judaism: Genesis verse 25:23, which refers to Esau and Jacob, states: "And the LORD said to her (Rebecca), "Two nations are in your womb, and two peoples born of you shall be divided; the one shall be stronger than the other, the elder shall serve the younger." Tertullian interpreted this statements as the Jews being the older nation that had to serve the younger nation, the Christians (Adversus Iudaeos I,1). It was this typology that repeatedly resulted in the Jews being deprived of their rights.

Augustine of Hippo, 354 - 430 AD, wrote the frequently quoted sentence: "Novum Testamentum in Vetere latet, et in Novo Vetus patet" ("The New Testament is hidden in the Old Testament, and the Old Testament is revealed in the New Testament." Quaestiones in Heptateuchum 2,73).

In his work "The City of God" (18,46) Augustine writes: "...Therefore, when they do not believe our Scriptures, their own, which they blindly read, are fulfilled in them, lest perchance any one should say that the Christians have forged these prophecies about Christ which are quoted under the name of the sibyl, or of others, if such there be, who do not belong to the Jewish people. For us, indeed, those suffice which are quoted from the books of our enemies, to whom we make our acknowledgment, on account of this testimony which, in spite of themselves, they contribute by their possession of these books, while they themselves are dispersed among all nations, wherever the Church of Christ is spread abroad. For a prophecy about this thing was sent before in the Psalms, which they also read, where it is written:[52] 'My God, His mercy shall prevent me. My God has shown me concerning mine enemies, that **You shall not slay them, lest they should at last forget Your law: disperse them in Your might.**' Therefore God has shown the Church in her enemies the Jews the grace of His compassion, since, as says the apostle, their offense[53] is the salvation of the Gentiles.' (Romans 11:11) And therefore He has not slain them, that is, He has not let the knowledge that they are Jews be lost in them, although they have been conquered by the Romans, lest they should forget the law of God, and their testimony should be of no avail in this matter of which we treat. But it was not enough that he should say, **Slay them not, lest they should at last forget Your law,** unless he had also added, **Disperse them**; because if they had only been in their own land with that testimony of the Scriptures, and not every where, certainly the Church which is everywhere could not have had them as witnesses among all nations to the prophecies which were sent before concerning Christ."

"They (the Jews) bear a mark of Cain[54] on their forehead".[55]

This opinion expressed by Augustine characterized Christology for a long time. Even Blaise Pascal (1623 -1662 AD) noted in Pensées: "(...) and it (the

Jewish people) have continued to exist in order to prove it (Christianity), and it must be in misery because they crucified him."[56]

During the massacre of the Jewish population in the Rhine region by crusaders in 1096, some people voiced the opinion that Jews should be placed on a par with Muslims, as infidels, in order to justify the atrocities. The theological justification claimed that the view held by Augustine in respect of the Jews' usefulness for proving the truth of the Christian doctrine was no longer applicable because the Jews had disregarded the original wording of the Hebrew Bible in favor of the Talmud. As such, "Slay them not" had become obsolete.

In keeping with tradition, Augustine wrote in his tractate "Adversus Iudaeos" (PL 42, 5. 27 et seq) that only the church can be seen as the "true Israel". In late antiquity, such views were not uncommon among church fathers: In the "Dialogus Christiani et Judaei" 45 from the 5th or 6th century AD, the supersession of Judaism by Christianity is derived from words spoken by the prophet Jeremiah: "The days are surely coming, says the LORD, when I will make a new covenant with the house of Israel and the house of Judah. It will not be like the covenant that I made with their ancestors when I took them by the hand to bring them out of the land of Egypt – a covenant that they broke, though I was their husband, says the LORD. But this is the covenant that I will make with the house of Israel after those days, says the LORD: I will put my law within them, and I will write it on their hearts; and I will be their God, and they shall be my people" (Jer 31:31-33 NRS).

It was not until the Second Vatican Council from 11 October 1962 to 8 December 1965 that a declaration about the relationship of the church to non-Christian religions was recorded, in NOSTRA AETATE, chapter 4: "God holds the Jews most dear for the sake of their Fathers; He does not repent of the gifts He makes or of the calls He issues-such is the witness of the Apostle."[57]

In doing so, the church followed the words of Paul: "God has not rejected his people whom he foreknew" (Rom 11:2 NRS); "... remember that it is not you that support the root, but the root that supports you" (Rom 11:18 NRS). As such, the church revoked its doctrine of many centuries of being the only "true Israel".

Chapter 4 of NOSTRA AETATE also states the following in reference to the Hebrew Bible's significance for Christianity: "She professes that all who believe in Christ-Abraham's sons according to faith[58] are included in the same Patriarch's call, and likewise that the salvation of the Church is mysteriously foreshadowed by the chosen people's exodus from the land of bondage. The Church, therefore, cannot forget that she received the revelation of the Old Testament through the people with whom God in His inexpressible mercy concluded the Ancient Covenant. Nor can she forget that she draws sustenance from the root of that well-cultivated olive tree onto which have been grafted the wild shoots, the Gentiles."

101

In doing so, the Council supported the exegesis of bible scholars for whom typology represented a mystery.

In the Theological Real Encyclopedia[59], Stuart George Hall provides an overview of the commentaries by leading theologians on typology. He lists a number of theologians who feel that typology represents an important element for understanding Christianity and therefore only analyze the Hebrew Bible from the perspective of the New Testament. I would like to highlight two deviating comments:

Karl Gustav Adolf Harnack, (1851– 1930) an important protestant theologian, believed that the Old Testament was of no relevance for the New Testament.[60] In 2007, Pope Benedict XVI voiced the opinion that Harnack as a theologian was trying to complete the work of Marcion the Heretic (85–160), which was to cut all ties of Christianity to the Old Testament.[61]

Jewish theologian Marc H. Ellis (* 1952) sees typology as a means of understanding, not the Hebrew Bible, but the New Testament.[62]

Hall ascertained the following about the findings of his research: "The typology should therefore be still used as an appropriate educational approach, but without the right to charge only the "true" or single meaning of the text ".

31. Epilogue

Following the examination of the differing beliefs that emerged between Christianity and Judaism, especially in the first two centuries CE, the material differences that separate these two religions from each other today are addressed below, bearing in mind the fact that both religions have groups that deviate in some articles of their respective faith.

31.1 The term "God"

Both religions see God as the highest instance in the world. We could therefore put the God of Israel on a par with the Christian God the Father. What separates the two is the Christian belief in the Trinity and, especially, in the belief that Jesus is the Son of God. The person of Jesus as part of the term "God" is not easy for Christians to explain since, according to the Council of Chalcedon in 451 AD:

"We, ...confess one and the same Son, our Lord Jesus Christ, the same perfect in Godhead and also perfect in manhood; truly God and truly man, of a reasonable [rational] soul and body; consubstantial [co-essential] with the Father according to the Godhead, and consubstantial with us according to the Manhood; in all things like unto us, without sin;

Begotten before all ages of the Father according to the Godhead, and in these latter days, for us and for our salvation, born of the Virgin Mary, the Mother of God, according to the Manhood;

one and the same Christ, Son, Lord, only begotten, to be acknowledged in two natures, inconfusedly, unchangeably, indivisibly, inseparably; the distinction of natures being by no means taken away by the union, but rather the property of each nature being preserved, and concurring in one Person and one Subsistence, not parted or divided into two persons, but one and the same Son, and only begotten God (μονογενῆ Θεὸν), the Word, the Lord Jesus Christ;"

The problem lies in the assumption of the Trinity, since various parts of mankind can be perceived in the one God but all must be of the same nature since otherwise there would not be one God. Since, however, according to "Chalcedon", Jesus is worshipped in "two natures, inconfusedly, unchangeably, indivisibly, inseparably", only the divine part can be included in the Trinity, in spite of this verdict of unity. The problem is overcome by assuming three persons who form the divine Trinity since the definition of the persons is vague in some respects.

Such partial elements of a single God are not unknown in Judaism. The religion also has a holy ghost and the Shekhinah, as mentioned above. The latter expression appears in the Talmud and means the presence of God, albeit with the addition "as if this were at all possible". When using the term Shekhinah for the presence of God, the Rabbis wanted to avoid this term being understood as a second deity. Centers of power in the divinity are also perceived in the Kabbalah. The terms Middat ha-Din and Middat ha-Rahamim were used to define the judging and merciful God, when describing God's action towards mankind before the court of divine judgment. The first term designates the judgment on the grounds of legality, i.e., the strict law, while the second term expresses God's mercy.

31.2 Jesus, the Messiah

As already mentioned, the term "Messiah ben Joseph" or "Messiah ben Ephraim" exists in Judaism to describe the coming of a Messiah. This Messiah is, however, not up to the task and is therefore killed. The Messiah ben David is expected next. The anticipated return of Jesus as the Redeemer can be equated to Israel's anticipation of a Messiah ben Judah.

31.3 The worship of Jesus

It is inconceivable for Jews to worship a deity who has previously lived as a human and has the same nature as humans as this would contradict the Jewish concept of monotheism. A distinction must be made, however, for requests for God's intercession, which, in Judaism, were asked by patriarchs or by Elijah. Examples of this include praying at Rachel's Tomb or in the Grotto of Elijah near Haifa, or pilgrimages to the tombs of highly respected Rabbis, which is especially typical of Moroccan-Jewish tradition.

31.4 Belief in afterlife

There is no difference between the Christian and the Jewish anticipation of an afterlife, since both religions believe in the resurrection of the body at the end of time.[65] Christianity does not equate the heavenly body with the earthly body, whereas orthodox Judaism believes in the resurrection of the earthly body.

31.5 Heavenly beings

Orthodox Jews, above all, and Christians believe in heavenly beings, such as angels or Elijah and Enoch. The last two could return to earth since – according to the literal interpretation of the Hebrew Bible – they ascended to God without dying first. Christians of a certain religious orientation also include Mary, the mother of Jesus, and saints among these beings. Prayers are addressed to them as mediators to God. Jews only address their prayers to God.

32. Bibliography

Attridge, Harold W., The Epistle of the Hebrews and the scrolls, in Avery-Peck, Alan J, When Judaism and Christianity Began: Essays in Memory of Anthony J. Saldarini, Leiden 2004, 315-342.

Augustinus, Aurelius, zweiundzwanzig Bücher über den Gottesstaat. Aus dem Lateinischen übers. von Alfred Schröder. (Des heiligen Kirchenvaters Aurelius Augustinus ausgewählte Schriften 1-3, Bibliothek der Kirchenväter, 1. Reihe, Band 01, 16, 28) Kempten; München 1911-16.

Baltzer, Klaus, Die Biographie der Propheten, Neukirchen-Vluyn 1975.

Bauckham, Richard, The Fate of the Dead, Studies on the Jewish and Christian Apokalypses, Heidelberg 1964.

Baumotte, Manfred, Die Frage nach dem historischen Jesus, Texte aus drei Jahrhunderten, Gütersloh 1984.

Boccaccini, Gabriele, (Hg.) 1. Enoch and the Messiah Son of Man: Revisiting the Book of Parables, Grand Rapids 2007

Bonz, Marianne Palmer, The Jewish Donor Inscriptions from Aphrodisias: Are they both Third-Century, and who are the Theosebeis?, in Harvard Studies in Classical Philology 96 (1994) 281-299.

Borgen, Peder, Philo of Alexandria, an exegete for his time, Leiden 1997.

Botermann, Helga, Griechisch-jüdische Epigraphik, in Zeitschrift für Papyrologie und Epigraphik 98 (1993) 184 - 121.

Bornkamm, Günther, Studien zum Matthäus-Evangelium, Neukirchen-Vluyn 2009.

Boyarin, Daniel, Border lines <dt.> |Abgrenzungen |die Aufspaltung des Judäo-Christentums, Berlin 2009.

Brugger, Eveline, Die Wehen des Messias, Berlin 2001.

Budge, E. A. Wallis, The Book of the Cave of Treasures, translated from the Syriac, London 1927.

Cavallin, Hans C., Leben nach dem Tode im Spätjudentum und im frühen Christentum, I. Spätjudentum, in Aufstieg und Niedergang der römischen Welt, II

Chiala, Sabino, Libro delle Parabole di Enoch, Brescia 1997.

Chilton, Bruce, James and the (Christian) Pharisees, in Avery-Peck, Alan J, When Judaism and Christianity Began: Essays in Memory of Anthony J. Saldarini, Leiden 2004, 18 - 47.

Chrysostomus, Johannes, La divine liturgie de S. Jean Chrysostome, Rom 1986.

Collins, Adela Yarbro, King and Messiah as Son of God, Grand Rapids, Mich. 2008

Collins, John J. [Hrsg.] The origins of apocalypticism in judaism and christianity, New York NY 1998.

Collins, John James, the Messiahs of the Dead Sea Scrolls and other ancient literature, New York NY 1995.

Conzelmann, Hans, Geschichte des Urchristentums, Göttingen 1983.

Danz, Christian [Hrsg.] Zwischen historischem Jesus und dogmatischem Christus, zum Stand der Christologie im 21. Jahrhundert, Tübingen 2010.

Denis, Albert-Marie, Introduction aux Pseudépigraphes grecs d'Ancien 'Testament, Leiden 1970.

Döpp, Siegmar [Hrsg.] Lexikon der antiken christlichen Literatur, Freiburg im Breisgau 2002.

Fabry, Heinz-Josef, Im Brennpunkt: Die Septuaginta, Studien zur Entstehung und Bedeutung der griechischen Bibel, Stuttgart 2002.

Flusser, David, Judaism of the Second Temple period, Bd.1 und 2, Grand Rapids, Mich. 2007- 2009.

Flusser, David, Bemerkungen eines Juden zur christlichen Theologie, München 1984, in Abhandlungen zum christlich-jüdischen Dialog Nr. 16.

Frankemölle, Hubert, Der Jude Jesus und die Ursprünge des Christentums, Mainz am Rhein 2003.

Hall, Stuart George, Typologie, in: Theologische Realenzyklopädie 34 (2002), S. 208-224.

Hare, Douglas, How Jewish ist he Gospel of Matthew?, in Catholic Biblical Quaterly 62 (2000) 264-277.

Hengel, Martin, Die Zeloten: Untersuchungen zur jüdischen Freiheitsbewegung in der Zeit von Herodes I. bis 70 n. Chr., Leiden 1961.

Hengel, Martin, Judentum und Hellenismus, Tübingen 1969.

Hoffmann, Andreas Gottlieb, (Übers. u. Hersg.) Das Buch Henoch, May, 2003. [Etext #4013]

Hollander, Harm W., und de Jonge, Marinus, The Testament of the Twelve Patriarchs, Leiden 1985.

Horseley, Richard, A., The Pharisees and Jesus in Galilee and Q, in Hurtado, Larry W., How on earth did Jesus become a god? Historical questions about earliest devotion to Jesus, Grand Rapids, Mich. 2006.

Hurtado, Larry W., Lord Jesus Christ: Avery-Peck, Alan J, When Judaism and Christianity Began: Essays in Memory of Anthony J. Saldarini ,Leiden 2004, 117-145. Devotion to Jesus in the Earliest Christianity, Grand Rapids 2003.

Hurtado, Larry W., One God, One Lord. Early Christian Devotion and Ancient Jewish Monotheism, Philadelphia 1988.

Josephus Flavius, Der Jüdische Krieg und Kleinere Schriften. Übersetzt und mit Einleitung und Anmerkungen versehen von Heinrich Clementz, Wiesbaden 2005.

Josephus Flavius, Jüdische Altertümer. Übersetzt und mit Einleitung und Anmerkungen versehen von Heinrich Clementz. Wiesbaden 2004.

Lohfink, Gerhard, Die Himmelfahrt Jesu, Untersuchungen zu den Himmelfahrts- und Erhöhungstexten bei Lukas, München 1979.

Marcus Joel, John the Baptist and Jesus, in Avery-Peck, Alan J, When Judaism and Christianity Began: Essays in Memory of Anthony J. Saldarini, Leiden 2004, 179-197.

Murphy, Frederick J., The Jewishness of Matthew, in Avery-Peck, Alan J, When Judaism and Christianity Began: Essays in Memory of Anthony J. Saldarini, Leiden 2004, S. 377-403.

Oegema, Gerbern S., Der Gesalbte und sein Volk, Untersuchungen zum Konzeptualisierungsprozeß der messianischen Erwartungen von den Makkabäern bis Bar Koziba, Göttingen 1994.

Pascal, Blaise, bearbeitet von Lafuma, Louis, Pensées sur la religion et sur quelques autres sujets, |Avant-propos et notes, Paris 1960.

Philonenko-Sayar, Belkis und Philonenko, Marc, Die Apokalypse Abrahams, Gütersloh 1982.

Piccirillo, Michele, The Mosaics of Jordan, Amman 1993.

Sanders, Ed Parish, Judaism: practice and belief; 63 BCE - 66 CE, London 2005[2].

Sanders, Ed Parish, Sohn Gottes: eine historische Biographie Jesu, Stuttgart 1996.

Schäfer, Peter, Die Geburt des Judentums aus dem Geist des Christentums, Tübingen 2010.

Schiffman, Lawrence H., The Dead Sea scrolls fifty years after their discovery, proceedings of the Jerusalem Congress, July 20 - 25, 1997, Jerusalem 2000.

Schubert, Kurt, Die Entwicklung der Auferstehungslehre von der nachexilischen bis zur frührabbinischen Zeit, in BZ 6 (1962) 177-214.

Segal, Alan F. Paul the convert, the apostolate and apostasy of Saul the Pharisee, New Haven 1990.

Segal, Allan F., Haevenly Ascent in Hellenistic Judaism, Early Christianity and their Environment, in Aufstieg und Niedergang der römischen Welt II 23.2, 1333-1394.

Stegemann, Wolfgang, Jesus und seine Zeit, Stuttgart 2010, in Biblische Enzyklopädie Nr. 10.

Stegemann, Wolfgang, Biblische Enzyklopädie 10. Jesus und seine Zeit. Stuttgart 2010.

Tobin, Thomas, S.J., Logos, in ABD 4, New York 1992, 348-56.

Udoh, Fabian E., Redefining first-century Jewish and Christian identities: essays in honor of Ed Parish Sanders, Notre Dame, Ind. 2008.

Van der Horst, Pieter, W., Hellenism – Judaism – Christianity, Kampen 1994.

Weinfeld, Moshe, Deuteronomy, in Enc. Jud., Jerusalem 1972, Bd. 5. Sp. 1582.

Wilamowitz-Moellendorff, Ulrich von, Der Glaube der Hellenen, Darmstadt 19943.

Witherington, Ben, The Jesus quest, the third search for the Jew of Nazareth, Downers Grove, Ill. 1995.

Wohlmuth, Josef, Die Tora spricht die Sprache der Menschen, theologische Aufsätze und Meditationen zur Beziehung von Judentum und Christentum, Paderborn 2002.

33. Abbreviations of the Books of the Bible

33.1. The Hebrew Bibel or the Old Testament

Genesis, Gen—Bereshith (תי ׳ שא.ר. ב·)
Exodus, Exo—Shemot (ת׳ומ ׳ ש)
Leviticus, Lev—Vayikra (א.ר.ק.י·.ו)
Numbers, Num—Bamidbar (ר.·ב.ד.מ. ב·)
Deuteronomy, Deu.-. Devarim (סיר.ב. ד·)
Joshua, Jos—Yehoshua
Judges, Jdg—Shoftim
Samuel, includes First and Second 1Sa–2Sa
Kings, includes First and Second, 1Ki–2Ki
Isaiah, Isa—Yeshayahu
Jeremiah, Jer—Yirmiyahu
Ezekiel, Eze—Yekhezkel
Hosea, Hos—Hoshea
Joel, Jol—Yoel
Amos, Amo—Amos
Obadiah, Oba—Ovadyah
Jonah, Joh—Yonah
Micah, Mic—Mikhah
Nahum, Nah—Nahum
Habakkuk, Hab—Havakuk
Zephaniah, Zep—Tsefanya
Haggai, Hag—Khagay
Zechariah, Zec—Zekharyah
Malachi, Mal—Malakhi
Psalms, Psa—Tehillim
Proverbs, Pro—Mishlei
Job, Job—Iyyov
Song of Songs, Sos—Shir ha-Shirim
Ruth, Rut—Rut
Lamentations, Lam—Eikhah
Ecclesiastes, Ecc—Kohelet

Esther, Est—Ester
Daniel, Dan—Daniel
Ezra, Eza, Ezra
Nehemiah, Neh—,Nehemiah
Chronicles, includes First and Second, 1Ch–2Ch—Divrei ha-Yamim (םימיה ירבד),
also called Divrei (ירבד)

33.2. The New Testament

Mat	The Gospel according to Matthew
Mar	The Gospel according to Mark
Luk	The Gospel according to Luke
Joh	The Gospel according to John
Apg	The Acts of the Apostles
Rom	The Letter to the Romans
1 Cor	The First Letter to the Corinthians
2 Cor	The Second Letter to the Corinthians
Gal	The Letter to the Galatians
Eph	The Letter to the Ephesians
Phil	The Letter to the Philippians
Col	The Letter to the Colossians
1Thess	The First Letter to the Thessalonians
2Thess	The Second Letter to the Thessalonians
1Tim	The First Letter to Timothy
2Tim	The Second Letter to Timothy
Tit	The Letter to Titus
Hebr	The Letter to the Hebrews
1Pe	The First Letter to Peter
2Pe	The Second Letter to Peter
1Jo	The First Letter to John
2Jo	The Second Letter to John
Apc	The Apocalypse of John (Revelation of John)
Eph	The Letter to the Ephesians
Tit	The Letter to Titus

33.3. Non-canonical Books

Tobit
Judith
1 Maccabees
2 Maccabees
Wisdom of Solomon
Sirach also called Ecclesiasticus
Baruch

33.4. Pseudepigraphic Books

PsS	Psalms of Salomon
1En	The Ethiopian Book of Enoch

33.5. Works of Philo

agr.	De acricultura (On Husbandry)
cher.	De Cherubim (On the Cherubim)
fug.	De fuga et inventione (On Flight and Finding)
gig.	De gigantibus (On the Giants)
her.	Quis rerum divinarum heres sit (Who is the Heir of Divine Things?)
migr.	De migratione Abrahami (On the Migration of Abraham)
mut.	De mutatione nominum (On the Change of Names)
post.	De posteritate Caini (On the Posterity of Cain and His Exile)
QG	Quaestiones in Genesim (Questions and Answers on Genesis I II III)
somn.	De somniis (On Dreams I-II)
spec.	De specialibus legibus (The Special Laws I II III IV)

33.6.   Abbreviations of Rabbinical Books

M.Mak	The Tractate Makot in the Mishnah
TSota	The Tractate Sota in the Tosephta
ySchek	The Tractate Shekalim in the Palestinian Talmud.
bPes	The Tractate Pesachim in the Babylonian Talmud

33.7 Professional Books

ABD	David Noel Freedman (ed.), The Anchor Bible Dictionary, New York 1992.
BZ	Biblische Zeitschrift (Bible Magazine)
CJ	The Classical Journal
GCS	Griechische christliche Schriftsteller (Greek Christian writers); Harnack, Adolf von, Protokollbuch der Kirchenväter-Kommission der Preußischen Akademie der Wissenschaften 1897 – 1928 (Journal of the Church Fathers' Commission of the Prussian Academy of Sciences).
PG	J.-P. Migne (ed.), Patrologia cursus completus Series graeca
PL	J.-P. Migne (ed.), Patrologia cursus completus Series prima [latina],
RGG⁴	Religion in Geschichte und Gegenwart (Religion past and present)
TRE	Theological Real Encyclopedia

33.8 Other Abbreviations

Cn.	Canon(s)

34. Register

Aaron 24, 32, 33, 44.
Abraham 46, 52, 65, 70, 71, 87, 89, 98, 99, 101.
Amidah 86.
Amos 15, 16, 21.
Angel 6, 8, 12, 14, 16, 17, 18, 19, 20, 26, 28, 30, 33, 42, 44, 49, 52, 53, 55, 68, 105.
Anthropology 64, 120.
Anthropomorphism 11.
Antichrist 84.
Apocalypse/Apokalyptic 5, 12, 15, 16, 17, 18, 20, 35, 47, 64, 68, 107, 120.
Apocalypse of Abraham 64.
Apocalypse of Zephaniah 64.
Apostolic Council 78, 79, 80, 81.
Archangel 47, 67.
Ark 11, 14.
Ashera 11.
Assyrians 15.
Augustine 7, 49, 100, 101.
Baal 11.
Babylon 11, 21, 41, 69.
Balaam 9.
Bar Kochba 59.
Barabbas 58.
Barnabas 79, 80.
Bauckham 64, 106, 120.
Bethlehem 23.
Bezalel 9, 27.
Book of Enoch 15, 18, 19, 20, 21, 22, 23, 28, 43, 64, 106, 107.

Book of Jubilees 64, 89, 120.
Caiaphas (high priest) 57.
Caligula 64.
Cassian 5.
Cavallin 65, 106, 120.
Cephas 79, 80, 84.
Chrysostomos 93, 96, 107, 121.
Circumcision 54, 78, 79, 90, 82, 83, 88, 92, 94, 95, 99.
Constantine I. (emperor) 92.
Constantinople 84.
Corinth 67.
Council of Chalcedon 103.
Daniel 19, 28, 63, 69.
David (king) 7, 21, 22, 23, 24, 39, 40, 41, 42, 46, 59, 72, 104.
Day of the Lord 15, 16, 47, 66, 68, 90.
Dead Sea 7, 107, 108.
Demiurge 3.
Didache 75.
Divine spirit 9, 10, 27.
Docetism 3.
Eden 64.
Egypt 3, 15, 25, 26, 47, 69, 101.
Elijah 44, 47, 60, 62, 66, 104, 105.
Ellis 102.
Elohim 9, 23, 24.
Enoch 16, 105
Epiphanius of Salamis 88.
Esau 100.
Essene 3.
Ezekiel 16, 19, 28.

35.   List of Figures

36. Acknowledgement

I would like to express my sincere gratitude to Professor Günter Stemberger for his kind willingness to read my manuscript and add his comments. I have incorporated some of his comments into the manuscript; others are included in the end notes.

37. Endnotes

1 Partly taken from Wikipedia: "Biblical exegesis".
2 Henotheism describes the belief in one superior God. Unlike the monotheism practised by Abrahamic religions, however, this belief does not automatically exclude the worship of other, lesser deities.
3 "Deuteronomist" is assumed to be a school of group of bible scholars
4 Weinfeld, Deuteronomy, in: Enc. Jud. Vol V, Col. 1582.
5 Baltzer, Die Biographie der Propheten, p. 162.
6 This and the following quotes stem from that part of Book 1 Enoch that is known as the Book of Parables. The dating is taken from Boccaccini, Gabriele, (ed.) 1. Enoch and the Messiah Son of Man: Revisiting the Book of Parables, Grand Rapids 2007 and Chiala, Sabino, Libro delle Parabole di Enoch, Brescia 1997.
7 The "fear of the Lord" is an expression which replaces "conscience". The Hebrew word for conscience "maspun" does not occur in the Bible.
8 Chapters 40 to 55 of the Book of Isaiah are attributed to a post-exilic prophet who was given the name of Deutero-Isaiah.
9 Comment from Prof. Stemberger: Similar Rabbinical statement: "The Sabbath is there for the people." See Mekhilta Shabbeta 1 to Ex 31,12: "The Sabbath was given to you and not you to the Sabbath" (bYoma 85b is virtually identical).
10 This Rabbinical law relates to "Eruv", whereby carrying an object in an enclosed area is permitted on the Sabbath. We cannot say with certainty how this rule was handled in Jesus' day. Even in the Mishnah, the Eruvin tractate (2nd order, 2nd tractate) is devoted to the Eruv. According to it, carrying certain objects was permitted in an area enclosed by a fence (real or symbolic).
11 The New Revised Standard Bible (NRS) first appeared in 1989, and has received wide acclaim and broad support from academics and church leaders as a Bible for all Christians.
12 TSota 13:2 etc.
13 Comment from Prof. Stemberger: "According to Rabbinic belief, only the start of a new dynasty needed to be anointed, but not the son of a King." Cf. Sifra, Mekhilta. de Milluim 1,1 (Weiss 41b), bHor 11b and frequently: "A King who is the son of a King is not anointed. And why did they anoint Salomo: Because of his dispute with Adonija" (i.e. the succession to the throne was disputed)."
14 Isaac's name is derived from the Hebrew word for "laugh" since, apparently, when God prophesied the birth of a son to Abraham: 17 "Then Abraham fell on his face and laughed, and said to himself, "Can a child be born to a man who is a hundred years old? Can Sarah, who is ninety years old, bear a child?" (Gen 17:17 NRS).
15 According to Wikipedia: "original sin".
16 Origen: In Matthaeum P.G. 13, 1777 C and note 89.
17 Text of the British Museum ms. add. 25875.
18 The Book of the Cave of Treasures (m'arrat gazzê) by (from the school of) Ephraim the Syrian, translated from Syriac by E. A. Wallis Budge, London 1927.
19 According to Wikipedia: "Church of the Holy Sepulchre".

20 In his essay "Relecture in Psalm 110" (1991, p. 253), Rudolf Kilian voices the opinion that this original Kings' Psalm was given a messianic meaning through the addition of the 4th verse.

21 Comment from Prof. Stemberger: "A distinction should be made between nefesh and neshama, although nefesh is also always corporeal. In its basic interpretation, neshama can also simply mean breath or power of life; the separation of body and soul occurred relatively late and always represented a marginal phenomenon."

22 Hengel, Judentum und Hellenismus, p. 364. Im Ueberweg Lexikon "Die Philosophie der Antike", Vol. 4, p. 541, Zeno of Citium: Man's soul is made of fire, it is divine, corporeal, not eternal. See also Wilamowitz-Moellendorff, Glaube der Hellenen I, p. 370-378. Schubert, Die Entwicklung p. 204, indicates that the words translated as "soul" in the Hebrew Bible mean "a soul equipped with bodily functions". Lohfink, Die Himmelfahrt p. 53 and note 150: A life outside the body, as propagated in the anthropology of the Old Testament, is scarcely possible in the Jewish apocalypse. "The Greek philosophy of body-soul dualism only exerted very little influence in Judaism and was never really entirely accepted."

23 For example: 1 Eno 103,3 et seq about the souls of the deceased pious, who will encounter "good, joy and honour".

24 For example: Book of Jubilees, 23,31: "And their bones shall rest in the earth. And their spirits will rejoice, and they will see that it is the Lord who is judging them..."

25 For example: Test. Dan 5,11: "And he shall take the captured [souls] from Beliar. And he shall convert the disobedient hearts to the Lord." Hollander, The Testament, p. 85, believes that the Book originated from Jewish sources, but was later edited by Christians some time up to the second half of the 2nd century, by which time it already approximated the version we know today.

26 Schubert, Das Problem, p. 158 et seq.

27 Bruns expresses the same opinion in Lexikon der antiken christlichen Literatur, p. 635.

28 Bauckham, The Fate, p. 91. (No other book mentions this apocalypse!)

29 It is assumed to have emerged some years after 70 AD. Philonenko-Sayar, Die Apokalypse Abrahams, p. 419.

30 Segal, Heavenly Ascent, p. 1362 et seq.

31 Denis, Introduction, p. 121, refers to Schürer and others who unanimously date the 4th Book in the period around 80 AD.

32 Lohfink, Die Himmelfahrt, p. 53.

33 Borgen, Philo, p.194-198.

34 The Pharisees (lat. pharisæ|us, -i; from heb.perushim/ parush, meaning "set apart" [1]) were at various times a political party, a social movement, and a school of thought among Jews during the Second Temple period under the Hasmonean dynasty (140 - 37 BCE). They were followed by Rabbinic Judaism.

35 Ebd. III, 362.

36 Cavallin, Leben, p. 307; Friedo Ricken, Seele I. Antike, in Historisches Wörterbuch Vol.9, col. 3: "The moral insight ... is understood as the soul encountering transcendental reality of the ideas, which requires the sublimation of the soul and its release from the body, which is only completed on death." Plato, Phaedo, 66 d 7-67 b 5; 79d 1-7; 82 b 10-d 7.

37 e.g.: No death without sin, bSchab 55a.

38 The non-canonical Book 2. Maccabees was composed about 124 BC. according to Harris, Stephen L., Understanding the Bible. Palo Alto: Mayfield. 1985.

39 Acts 24:15

40 Joh 5:28-29.

41 Mat 25:31,32,46.

42 See van der Horst, Pieter, W., Hellenism – Judaism – Christianity, Kampen 1994, p. 103.

43 From the "Internet Sacred Text Archive".

44 Comment from Prof. Stemberger: "These laws are also implied in Acts 15,19 et seq; more detail about their development can be found in Klaus Müller, Tora für die Völker, 1994."

45 Bonz, The Jewish Donor, p.53; Wander, Gottesfürchtige, 158 et seq.

46 This date takes the Deuteronomist "Letter of Paul to the Colossians" into consideration.

47 See van der Horst, Pieter, W., Hellenism – Judaism – Christianity, Kampen 1994, p. 102.

48 This was also the case in the Letters of Revelation 1,9-3,22.

49 Comment from Prof. Stemberger: "Mishnah Avoda Zara 1 also forbids Jews to celebrate with heretics".

50 Piccirillo, Michele, The Mosaics of Jordan, p. 39.

51 Chrysostomus, Johannes, La divine liturgie de S. Jean Chrysostome, Rome 1986, p. 61.

52 Psa 59,11 (King James Version).

53 Not recognising Jesus as the Messiah.

54 See Gen 4,15: "Then the Lord said to him, "Not so! Whoever kills Cain will suffer a sevenfold vengeance". And the Lord put a mark on Cain, so that no one who came upon him would kill him."

55 The last clause originates from the commentary on Psa 40.

56 Following editing by Louis Lafuma 311.

57 Cf. Rom. 11:28-29; cf. dogmatic Constitution, Lumen Gentium (Light of nations) AAS, 57 (1965) p. 20.

58 Cf. Gal. 3:7.

59 TRE 34 (2002), p. 208-224.

60 TRE 34 (2002), p. 217.

61 Benedict XVI.: Jesus of Nazareth. From the Baptism in the Jordan to the Transfiguration. Herder, 2007, p. 80 et seqq.

62 TRE 34 (2002), p. 217.

63 Comment from Prof. Stemberger: "This is also the most widespread rabbinical theory, although other ideas exist (cf. my essay "Zur Auferstehungslehre in der rabbinischen Literatur". Kairos, 15 (1973), 238-266, recently in more detail: José Costa, L'au-delà et la résurrection dans la littérature rabbinique ancienne, Paris 2004."

Die Wiener Vorlesungen laden seit 1987 wichtige Persönlichkeiten des intellektuellen Lebens dazu ein, in den Festsälen des Rathauses ihre Analysen und Befunde zu den großen aktuellen Problemen der Welt vorzulegen.

Anliegen der Wiener Vorlesungen ist eine Schärfung des Blicks für die Komplexität, Differenziertheit und – häufig auch – Widersprüchlichkeit der Wirklichkeit. Der analytisch-interpretative Zugang der Wiener Vorlesungen dämpft die Emotionen und legt Fundamente für eine Bewältigung der Probleme mit zivilen und demokratischen Mitteln. Das Publikum trägt durch seine Teilnahme an den Wiener Vorlesungen zur „Verbreitung jenes Virus" bei, das für ein gutes politisches Klima verantwortlich ist.

Bei den Wiener Vorlesungen waren seit 1987 über 1000 Vortragende aus allen Kontinenten zu Gast. Unter den Referenten befanden sich u. a. Marie Albu-Jahoda, Ulrich Beck, Bruno Bettelheim, Ernesto Cardenal, Carl Djerassi, Marion Dönhoff, Irenäus Eibl-Eibesfeldt, Manfred Eigen, Mario Erdheim, Amitai Etzioni, Vilem Flusser, Viktor Frankl, Peter Gay, Maurice Godelier, Ernst Gombrich, Michail Gorbatschow, Jeanne Hersch, Eric J. Hobsbawm, Werner Hofmann, Ivan Illich, Verena Kast, Otto F. Kernberg, Rudolf Kirchschläger, Václav Klaus, Ruth Klüger, Teddy Kollek, Kardinal Franz König, György Konrad, Bischof Erwin Kräutler, Bruno Kreisky, Peter Kubelka, Hermann Lübbe, Viktor Matejka, Adam Michnik, Hans Mommsen, Max F. Perutz, Hugo Portisch, Uta Ranke-Heinemann, Eva Reich, Marcel Reich-Ranicki, Horst-Eberhard Richter, Erwin Ringel, Carl Schorske, Edward Shorter, Helmut Sohmen, Marcel Tshiamalenga Ntumba, Paul Watzlawick, Georg Weidenfeld, Erika Weinzierl, Ruth Wodak, Hans Zeisel.

Die Reihe „Wiener Vorlesungen. Forschungen" bietet die Möglichkeit, wissenschaftliche Arbeiten, die durch die Wiener Vorlesungen eröffnet und angeregt wurden, einer größeren Öffentlichkeit vorzustellen.

Wiener Vorlesungen:
Forschungen

Herausgegeben für die Kulturabteilung der Stadt Wien
von Hubert Christian Ehalt

Band 1   Julian Uher: Systembedingte Arbeitslosigkeit – alternative Beschäftigungspolitik. 2000.

Band 2   Michael Lang: Die Rechtsprechung des EuGH zu den direkten Steuern. Welcher Spielraum bleibt den Mitgliedstaaten? 2007.

Band 3   Wolfgang Neugebauer / Kurt Scholz / Peter Schwarz (Hrsg.): Julius Wagner-Jauregg im Spannungsfeld politischer Ideen und Interessen – eine Bestandsaufnahme. Beiträge des Workshops vom 6. / 7. November 2006 im Wiener Rathaus. 2008.

Band 4   Peter Landesmann: Der Antijudaismus auf dem Weg vom Judentum zum Christentum. 2012.

Band 5   Peter Landesmann: Anti-Judaism on the Way from Judaism to Christianity. 2012.

www.peterlang.de

Bartosz Adamczewski

Heirs of the Reunited Church

The History of the Pauline Mission in Paul's Letters, in the So-Called Pastoral Letters, and in the Pseudo-Titus Narrative of Acts

Frankfurt am Main, Berlin, Bern, Bruxelles, New York, Oxford, Wien, 2010.
178 pp.
ISBN 978-3-631-60504-2 · hardback € 43,80*

The work establishes the relative and absolute chronology of Paul's life. It demonstrates that Paul went to Jerusalem only two times after his conversion. The second visit, which was planned in Rom and described retrospectively in Gal, ended up with the Antiochene conflict. The following Eucharistic schism within early Christianity has lasted for at least a century after Paul's death in AD 49. The so-called Pastoral Letters, which are in fact ethopoeic, confirm this state of matters. The history of the Pauline mission, as it was described in the Acts of the Apostles, is a result of sixfold hypertextual reworking of Gal 1:17-2:14; Rom 15:25-32 with the use of other Pauline and post-Pauline texts. Luke irenically described the history of early Christianity as a history of the reunited Church.

Content: Chronology of Paul's life as it may be deduced from Paul's own letters · Chronology of Paul's life as it is assumed in the so-called Pastoral Letters · Hypertextual reworking of the Pauline and post-Pauline letters in Acts

*The e-price includes German tax rate. Prices are subject to change without notice

Frankfurt am Main · Berlin · Bern · Bruxelles · New York · Oxford · Wien
Distribution: Verlag Peter Lang AG
Moosstr. 1, CH-2542 Pieterlen
Telefax 0041 (0)32/376 17 27
E-Mail info@peterlang.com

40 Years of Academic Publishing
Homepage http://www.peterlang.com